• *The Apocalypse*

The Apocalypse

ANDRÉ FEUILLET

alba house

STATEN ISLAND N.Y.

A DIVISION OF ST. PAUL PUBLICATIONS

Translated from the French by
Rev. Thomas E. Crane, S.S.L.
St. John Vianney Seminary
Diocese of Buffalo

Nihil Obstat: *Stanislaus J. Brzana, S.T.D.*
Censor Librorum

Imprimatur: ✠ *James C. McNulty*
Bishop of Buffalo

January 20, 1964

Library of Congress Catalog Card Number 65-15728

*Designed, printed and bound in the U.S.A. by the Pauline Fathers
and Brothers of the Society of St. Paul at Staten Island, New York
as part of their publishing apostolate.*

Copyright 1965 by Society of St. Paul, Staten Island, N. Y.

*Published originally by Desclée de Brouwer
under the title "L'Apocalypse."*

CONTENTS

INTRODUCTION

Of all the writings of the New Testament, the Apocalypse is doubtless the most difficult. Also, the interpretation of it has developed considerably throughout the centuries. For a long time writers considered it to be unique, not realizing how closely its literary form is related to the large number of non-inspired Jewish apocalypses which had been entirely unknown, until they began to be rediscovered in recent years.

J. B. Frey, in his article *Apocalyptique*, in *Supplement au Dictionnaire de la Bible,* tome I, cols. 326-354, gives a list of the writings belonging to the Jewish apocalyptic style, of the era contemporary to Jesus, as well as a descriptive study of the literary form. The Qumran writings, of course, have greatly increased our supply of relevant material. However, although no single Qumran text could be called an apocalypse strictly speaking, still we find the apocalyptic literary form scattered throughout these texts, especially in the *Rule of War* (which some writers hold to be an apocalypse), and in the *Hymns* and in the *Manual of Discipline,* etc.

Apocalyptic literature abounded from about 200 B.C. to about the end of the first century of the Christian era, after

which the Jews allowed their attention to be absorbed by the
study of the Law and of the legal elements of their ancient
traditions. Apocalyptic literature is basically an outgrowth of
the prophetic tradition, but having its own peculiar characteristics. Whereas the prophetic texts are the traditions of men
conscious of having been personally called by God, the
apocalyptic writings, on the other hand, are generally pseu-
donymous and attributed fictitiously to outstanding persons
of the distant past. The prophets were apostles, keenly aware
of their responsibility; apocalyptists were theorists and
dreamers. The prophets were fully immersed in the burning
problems of their own day, looking to the future only to
explain it, to console or to convert their contemporaries. The
apocalyptists look principally to the future, transporting their
readers into a dream-world of heroic proportions.

The striking originality of John's Apocalypse is in the
fact that, while he uses the style, imagery and method of
the Jewish apocalyptic tradition, he remains faithful nonetheless to the greatness of the ancient prophets. W. Hadorn,
in his commentary, (p. 8; cf. below), says, "if the hands
are those of Esau, the voice is that of Jacob." As did the
great prophets of the past, John names himself as author
at the beginning of his work, thus dissociating himself at
least from the practice of claiming pseudonymity. Like them,
however, he desires the salvation of his people (cf. the letters
of chapters 2-3), and wished to offer an answer to the burning
problems of his age.

John's Apocalypse was long thought to contain hidden
information about the future of the Church, especially
about the last days. Nowadays, however, it is appreciated
more for the light which it sheds upon the end of the first
century. Although there have been some exaggerations in
the shifting of opinions regarding the Apocalypse, still, it

remains essentially a prophetic book, as Christian tradition has always held it to be. We must simply be on guard against the tendency to require of its apostolic author more information than he intended to give, or insights which he had no thought of conveying.

Our study of the Apocalypse will proceed as follows: After considering the general tendencies of recent commentators, and the different interpretations which they offer (chapter I), we shall offer a study of the unity of composition and literary structure of the Apocalypse (chapter II); chapter III will study the interpretation of the Apocalypse as a whole, and chapter IV will present its doctrinal content; chapters V, VI, and VII will consider, respectively, the place and date of composition, the author, and some various specific problems.

CHAPTER I

GENERAL TENDENCIES OF RECENT COMMENTATORS: DIFFERENT METHODS OF INTERPRETATION

Even nowadays authors are far from agreed on how best to explain the Apocalypse. In an article published in *Ami du Clergé* (Tome 71, 1961) and entitled, *Les diverses méthodes d'interpretation de l'Apocalypse et les commentaires récents* (pp. 257-270) we presented a review of the different methods of interpretation which have been offered since the beginning up to the present. Throughout the course of the centuries they have fallen, in general, into the following types; the *millenary exegesis,* which was popular among the most ancient authors, especially Hippolytus; the system of *recapitulation,* which was characteristic of the outlook of no less an authority than St. Augustine (*City of God,* XX: 17; *the history of the universe,* which was popular toward the end of the Middle ages; the *eschatological* system and, that of the *application of the data of the Apocalypse to contemporary events both* of which were developed in the sixteenth century, as a reaction against the fanciful abstractions of the earlier interpreters; and finally the *documentary and comparative methods,* which have resulted from the scientific exegesis of the 19th and 20th centuries.

In these pages, we shall pass quickly in review the commentaries which have appeared in recent years, indicating to which of these systems they belong. We should bear in mind, however, that these methods seldom are perfectly pure; usually they are joined to one another, or to some different one, as example, the documentary method joined to the eschatological, or to a reference to mythology. The distinction of types, therefore, is more a question of emphasis than of strict separation.

We shall limit our study to the works produced since 1920, which was the date of the monumental work in 2 volumes of R. H. Charles, as part of the *International Critical Commentary; A Critical and Exegetical Commentary on the Revelation of St. John, with Notes and Indices* (Edinburgh). This masterpiece is remarkable for its careful attention to the minutest details of text, vocabulary, grammar, and of the structure and rhythm of the phrases. Charles seeks to explain the Apocalypse not only by the Bible, but also by other Jewish apocalyptic literature, which he knows admirably well.

As for interpretation, Charles has not so much a fixed method, as rather an inclination toward the *eschatological* school (of which we shall say more below). According to Charles, the Seer describes from beginning to end the events which are to mark the consummation of all things and the final triumph of God, according to a definite and constant chronological progression, except for some of the visions, (i.e. 7: 9-17; 10-11; 13; 14) which he considers to be proleptic.

However, it is more particularly on the level of literary analysis that Charles seeks to resolve the difficulties involved in the exegesis of the Apocalypse. Cf. also (by the same author) *Lectures on the Apocalypse*, (London, 1923). He is not favorable to the tendency to break up the Apocalypse into documents of different origins, (as are Völter; Vischer; Weyland; Spitta; Erbes; J. Weiss; Bousset, and others).

Rather, he tries to identify and date the different Greek and Jewish sources which John uses, in addition to the Old Testament. He is convinced, furthermore, that the obscurities of the actual text cannot be solved by the various systems, such as that of *recapitulation* (cf. below), but are due rather to the work of an unintelligent and incompetent disciple of the author, who has edited the original account of John's visions; this editor has, in effect, disfigured one of the most eloquent and noble works of the New Testament and, for that matter, of the entire Bible.

A year after Charles' commentary was published, there appeared that of E. B. Allo, *Saint Jean, L'Apocalypse* (Collection *Etudes Bibliques*. 4th edition, enlarged, Paris, 1933). From the point of view of philology, Allo's commentary is less rich than that of Charles. Still, Allo's excellent effort at explaining the text makes his work a milestone in the history of French and Catholic exegesis of the Apocalypse. Lavergne published an abridged edition of Allo's commentary, *L'Apocalypse,* Paris, 1930, Cf. also Allo's article *Apocalypse,* in SDB, Tome I, cols. 306-325.

Allo interprets the Apocalypse according to the theory of *recapitulation,* which was begun by Victorin of Pettau (cf. his commentary in *P.L.* 5; 281-344; and in the *Corpus Vindobonense,* 39), and the Donatist, Tyconius. (This latter's commentary was unfortunately lost, but it has been reconstructed in part, thanks to the efforts of later exegetes, such as example Primatius, Beatus of Liebana, and others.) According to this theory of recapitulation, the Apocalypse presents not a chronological succession of events but rather the same events, seen under a number of different aspects.

Shortly after Allo, in 1923, A. Loisy published *L'Apocalypse de Jean* (Paris), building his commentary according to the outlook of the school of *religionsgeschichte* or *tradition-sgeschichte*, which was born under the influence of H. Gunkel (*Schöpfung und Chaos in Urzeit und Endzeit*, Göttingen, 1903, reprinted in 1921, and *Zum religionsges-chichtlichen Verstaendnis des Neuen Testaments*, Goettin-gen, 1903, reprinted in 1930). This school explains the Apoca-lypse, at least partially, in terms of the influence of Greek and oriental pagan mythology. Loisy borrows especially from F. Boll, *Aus der Offenbarung Johannis, Hellenistische Stud-ien zum antiken Weltbild der Apokalypse*, (Leipzig, Berlin, 1914). Nonetheless, he clearly recognizes the specifically Christian character of the Apocalypse.

Gunkel seeks to explain the Apocalypse especially by appealing to the Babylonian myths: Bousset, in his valuable commentary (*Die Offenbarung Johannis, Göttingen* 1896-1906), appeals to Iranian traditions; Boll and Loisy refer especially to the astrology and astral myths of Hellenism. Lohmeyer, in his commentary, *Die Offenbarung des Johan-nes* (in *Handbuch zum Neuen Testament herausgegeben von H. Leitzmann* 1926; re-edited by G. Bornkamm after Loh-meyer's death in 1953), looks for sources in the Mandaean writings.

Thus, Lohmeyer's commentary also belongs, in a way, to the *traditionsgeschichtliche* school. However, Lohmeyer's chief concern is to defend the explanation of the Apocalypse offered by the eschatological school (*endeschichtlich*), inaugurated by the Spanish Jesuit Ribeira (*Commentarius in Apocalypsim*, Salamanca, 1591). According to Lohmeyer, all of the section of the Apocalypse from chapters 4-21, is eschatological; the enthronement of the lamb in chapter 5; birth of the Messiah in chapter 12; also the Babylonian woman is not at all related to the historical Rome, but is rather a diabolical representation of the invisible world.

Likewise, the two beasts of chapter 13, modeled after the Leviathan and Behemoth of the Old Testament, are diabolical without any relation to actual history. Thus to the eyes of the Apocalypse author, past, present, and future are in a way, interchangeable, which is to say that he sees salvation in the last analysis as an atemporal matter. Furthermore, Lohmeyer is not content to see the Apocalypse as a magnificent prose poem, (which is held by most); rather, he sees the whole text divided into strophes, or at least into verses. This hypothesis, if it could be demonstrated, would establish the absolute literary unity of the work.

Much less systematic is the commentary of W. Hadorn; *Die Offenbarung des Johannes*, (Leipzig, 1928), in *Theologischer Handkommentar zum Neuen Testament*. The author rejects, first of all, the pretended dependence on Mandaean texts. His interpretation is that John uses old ideas (thus Hadorn's hypothesis borrows from the school of Gunkel). Hadorn sees John as thinking, first of all, of pagan Rome, but at the same time, he sees the Seer as expressing the eternal truths. Thus, in this sense only, the explanation is at the same time *reichesgeschichtlich* and *endesgeschichtlich*. However, there should be no concrete application, or pretension to any actual prediction of historical events. It is simply that the Apocalypse exposes the fundamental laws which govern the Kingdom of God, and that it thus explains any epoch of history.

The very traditional commentary of Th. Zahn, *Die Offenbarung des Johannes* in 2 volumes, (Leipzig-Erlangen, 1924-1926), is eschatological, and also millenarian, like those of Papias and Irenaeus (cf. the last chapter). Its chief value lies in the profound study which Zahn has made of ancient Christian commentaries.

Notwithstanding some occasional interesting insights,

the commentary of Msgr. J. Blane, *Les Visions de saint Jean* (Paris, 1924) is somewhat superficial and apologetic in tone. The author presumes to translate the text into a rather mediocre French verse. In the same year, the Protestant Willemze published his commentary, *De Openbaring van Johannes* (Groningen), which is quite like that of Allo. The commentary of J. de Zwaan, *De Openbaring van Johannes*, (Haarlem, 1925), sees the Apocalypse as a missionary polemic against rampant paganism.

In 1928 Baldensperger published a brief commentary in the *Bible du Centenaire* (tome IV, pp. 413-440). His work reflects the views of the *eschatological* school. Unlike Lohmeyer, Baldensperger does not deny all historical allusions, although, according to him, John has no idea of a history as perduring; John announces only the end of the world, which he sees as imminent.

In 1937, J. du Plessis published a two volume work, *Les Derniers temps d'aprés l'Histoire et la Prophétie* (Paris), of which the second volume is devoted to the Apocalypse. His commentary is no more than a modernized rendering of the ideas of Joachim of Flores (*Expositio in Apocalypsim* (Venice, 1527), and in Nicholas of Lyre (*Postillae Perpetuae, sive Praevia Commentaria in universa Biblia* (Rome, 1471-1472), who see in the Apocalypse a *revelation of the history of the universe,* and of the seven ages of the Church. This method of interpretation can now be considered passé.

The commentary on the Apocalypse in the *Sainte Bible* compiled by Pirot and Clamer (Tome XII, Paris, pp. 581-667) was done by A. Gelin. The author follows the so called *historical* (*zeitgeschichtlich*) method, used especially by E. Renan in his *Antéchrist* (Paris, 1871), and by many commentators of the 17th century, especially Alcazar (*Vestigatio sensus Apocalypsis,* Antwerp, 1614-1619). This method consists of looking in the Apocalypse for allusions to the events of the second half of the first century of the Christian era. Gelin relies heavily in his commentary on the thesis of P. Touilleux, *L'Apocalypse et les cultes de Domitien et de Cybéle*, (Paris, 1935).

In a commentary published in 1939 and re-edited in 1942, *Erklärung der Johannesapokalypse*, (Bonn), J. Sickenberger strongly resists this *zeitgeschichtlich* method, and defends a purely *eschatological* exegesis, having no connection with contemporary history. From the opposite view M. Kiddle (*The Revelation of St. John; The Moffatt New Testament Commentary*, London, 1940, and re-edited often afterwards) holds that John sees the Church of his own day and describes the eschatological events according to the characteristics of the events of his own era. Very similar views were already expressed by J. Rohr in *Der Hebraerbrief und die Geheime Offenbarung des Heiligen Johannes* (in *Die Heilige Schrift des Neuen Testaments*, Bonn, 1932). This hypothesis appears in the work of E. F. Scott, *The Book of Revelation* (London, 1939), and in the commentary of E. Lohse, *Die Offenbarung des Johannes* (in *Das Neuen Testament Deutsch*, Band II, Göttingen, 1960) and in the work of J. Behm, *Die Offenbarung des Johannes*, Göttingen, 1949 (in *Das Neuen Testament Deutsch*); as are the Epistles of the New Testament, the Apocalypse is a work designed to be read not by unborn future generations, but by the faithful of a definite period of time, the era present to the author; nonetheless, it is at the same time a prophetic work, giving, to Christians of all eras, certitude in the eventual victory of the Kingdom of God.

The Protestant pastor, P. de Benoit has produced *Ce que l'Ésprit dit aux Eglises, Commentaire de l'Apocalypse*, (Venne sur Lausanne, 1941); this work however, is merely popular, as is that of Canon van der Heeren, *L'Apocalypse ou le Livre de la Révélation de saint Jean* (Bruges, 1941). After his shorter work on the meaning of the Apocalypse (*Der Sinn der Apokalypse des hl. Johannes*, Münster i. W. 1931), A. Wikenhauser published his *Offenbarung des Johannes übersetzt und erklärt* in the *Regensburger Neues Testament*, (Regensburg, 1947; 3rd edition, 1959). In this latter work, Wikenhauser sees the Apocalypse as the Book of Daniel of the New Testament. According to this hypothesis, the author takes his lead from Daniel and also from the eschatological discourses of Jesus (Mk. 13 and parallel texts), and then goes on to describe the various phases of the eschatological drama, not without allowing himself (as does the author of Daniel) to make a number of allusions to the history of his own era. In the prophecy of Jesus recorded in the Synoptics, contemporary history, such as the destruction of the temple, and of Jerusalem (*Zeitgeschichte*) and the perspective of the last things, i.e. the second coming of Christ (*Endgeschichte*) are inseparable.

Père M. E. Boismard wrote the fascicule of the *Bible de Jérusalem* on the Apocalypse (Paris, 1950; 3rd edition, revised, 1959). His annotated translation was preceded by several studies relative to the literary composition of the Apocalypse, (*L'Apocalypse ou les Apocalypses de saint Jean*, *Révue Biblique*, 1949, pp. 507-541; and *Notes sur l'Apocalypse* in *Revue Biblique*, 1952, pp. 161-181). The same author has contributed the section on the Apocalypse in *Introduction à la Bible*, compiled by A. Robert and A. Feuillet, Tome II, *Nouveau Testament*, Tournai, 1959, pp. 709-742. Père Boismard has no desire to revise the *documentary hypotheses* of the 19th century, which spoke of texts of different origins, joined by a redactor. Rather, he maintains that the style of the Apocalypse is peculiarly its own, and that therefore one hand must be responsible for the entire work. However, he holds that the same author wrote two similar works at two different times, and that eventually these two works were combined into one book. This would serve to explain the doublets and inconsistencies in composition.

Père J. Bonsirven's profound knowledge of Jewish literature made him eminently qualified to interpret the Apocalypse. However, his commentary in the collection *Verbum Salutis* (*L'Apocalypse de saint Jean*, Paris, 1951) fails to open any new paths. It was translated into Italian by U. Massi, as *L'Apocalisse di S. Giovanni*, (Rome, Studium, 1958). P. Bonsirven adheres strictly to the *recapitulation* theory, regarding as simultaneous the three septets of the seals, the trumpets and the bowls.

L'Apocalypse lue aux Chrétiens, of L. Cerfaux and J. Cambier, in the collection *Lectio divina* (Paris, 1955), is designed to make available to present day Christians the message of consolation which St. John addressed to his contemporaries caught in the throes of a rabid persecution. Just as the Seer of the Apocalypse continually uses the ancient Scriptures, which he very probably read in a Greek version similar to that of the Septuagint, so the Old Testament texts have been translated in the light of John's visions, of which the Old Testament visions are the prototypes. The interpretation of details allows considerable room for traditional symbolic imagery. Thus the work leans to the *recapitulation* theory, but without a definite system.

The commentary of Ch. Brütsch, *Clarté de l'Apocalypse*, Genêve, 1955, (abridged edition in the collection "*La Bible ouverte*"; *L'Apocalypse*, Neuchâtel-Paris, 1957), is a thorough re-working of the same author's original work, which appeared in 1930. Like Dr. Moffatt, Brütsch is convinced that "pastoral work is exactly the kind of preparation one needs most to be able to offer on effective commentary in the Apocalypse" (p. 12). In the light of this preparation, the author, who is a pastor, applies himself to the task of distilling the perduring religious meaning of the sacred text. The desire and thought-provoking footnotes and the excursus sections at the end of the work offer a considerable mass of information on the passages and problems which are most discussed.

The 22nd volume of the Montserrat Bible, *La Biblia Versio dels textos originals i Commentari pels monjos de Montserrat* (Abbaye de Montserrat, 1958), contains, besides a commentary on the Catholic Epistles especially done by R. M. Diaz, an explanation of the Apocalypse written by Dom Guiu M. Camps, (pp. 221-352). This commentary belongs to the *eschatological* school, insofar as it sees the coming of the Kingdom of God as the underlying theme of the Apocalypse; announcement of the coming of the King- dom (6: 1 - 11: 13); diabolical persecutions, designed to im- pede the coming of the kingdom, (11: 14 - 13: 18); divine judgment and retribution (14: 1 - 19: 21); the reign of 1000 years (20: 1 - 15); the new Jerusalem (21 - 22).

The collection *"Bibliothèque Historique"* of Payot, con- tains a translation by J. L. Pidoux of a work by H. Lilye, Lutheran bishop of Hanover, *L'Apocalypse, le dernier livre de la Bible*, Paris, 1959. As is the preceding work, this com- mentary is of the *eschatological* school, according to which the Apocalypse is principally an announcement of the end of time and of the second coming of Christ.

Among the popular works are the following, which are of quite unequal value: Fortunatus of Valetta, *Apocalypse de s. Jean, Bref commentaire*, Ottawa, 1939; D. W. Richard- son, *The Revelation of Jesus Christ*, 1939; H. Mosbech,

Johannes Aabenbaring indledet og forklaret. Copenhagen, 1943; R. G. Loenertz, *The Apocalypse of Saint John,* London, 1947; E. Reissner, *Das Buch mit den sieben Siegeln,* Göttingen, 1949; R. H. Preston and A. T. Hanson *The Revelation of St. John the Divine* (The Torch Bible), London, 1949; A. Schlatter, *Die Briefe und die Offenbarung des Johannes,* Stuttgart, 1950; A. von Speyr, *Apokalypse, Betrachtungen zur Geheimen Offenbarung,* 2 vol., Einsiedeln, 1950; H. Frey, *Das Ziel aller Dinge* Stuttgart, 1953; E. Schick, *Die Apokalypse* in *Echter-Bibel,* Würzburg, 1952; P. Häring, *Die Botschaft der Offenbarung des Heiligen Johannes,* Munich, 1953; P. Ketter, *Die Apokalypse,* in *Die Heilige Schrift für das Leben erklärt,* Freiburg, 1953; Thomas S. Kayler, *The Book of Revelation,* New York - Oxford, 1957; E. Bernett and L. H. Hough in *The Interpreter's Bible,* vol. XII, New York - Nashville, 1957; J. W. Bowmann, *The Drama of the Book of Revelation,* Philadelphia (no date); M. Planque, *Introduction à l'Apocalypse,* Colmar - Paris, 1959: selected passages arranged to serve as a first introduction to the Apocalypse; O. Moe, *Bibelens siste bok. En utlegning av Johannes' openbaring,* Oslo, 1960; J. B. Smith, *A Commentary on the Book of Revelation, A Revelation of Jesus Christ,* Scottdale, 1961.

CHAPTER II

UNITY OF COMPOSITION AND LITERARY STRUC-TURE OF THE APOCALYPSE

The two questions of unity of composition and of the literary structure cannot be studied separately, since they deal with the same basic element of the Apocalypse's internal literary order. Our study will consider first the opinions of the various commentators, as we listed them in the foregoing chapter; then we shall see the writings which they have dedicated to these problems; finally we shall offer our own personal opinion, by way of conclusion. (This will be the plan for the succeeding chapters as well.)

Commentaries

Charles undertook a study of the Apocalypse which was too detailed to allow him not to become aware of the fact that the unity of language and of style render unlikely any pretensions of the *Literarkritiker*. However, he proceeds nevertheless, with disconcerting self assurance, and presumes to identify and to date what he considers to be the many and varied sources which John has used. He offers, for example, such conclusions as the following:- 7: 1-8 comes from a Jewish or Jewish - Christian source redacted before 70, because the listing of the tribes must be concerned with Israel according to the flesh, and not in the spiritual sense which would prevail after the destruction of the center of the nation's earthly unity; 11: 1-2 predicts the preservation of the Temple and of those who adore in it (the Zealots, who stayed in the sanctuary during the siege); thus it must be a Jewish document from before 70. Likewise 11: 3-13, which sees Jerusalem as still standing. 12: 1-5, 13-17 are originally from a pagan source, as is proven by the mythological way in which Christ's existence is described, with no reference to His death or resurrection. On the other hand, 12: 7-10, 12 are Jewish. 17: 1c-2, 3b-6a, 7, 18 and 18: 2-25 are the work of a Jewish author of the time of Titus; whereas 17: 11-13 and 17: 16 are from a quietistic pharisee of before 70. The letters to the churches were written by the Seer in the time of Vespasian and incorporated later into his book.

Charles was also led by his own analytical method, to conclude to the intervention of an amazingly incompetent and uninformed editor. 1: 8 is a most ill-fitting addition, since John could not yet hear God's words until after he has gone into ecstasy in 1: 10. Originally chapter 8 contained only three curses; 8: 7-12 was added by the editors to bring the section to a septet; 14: 3c, 4ab is a non-Christian interpolation which logically excludes from the company of the followers of the Lamb all married persons and all women. In 14: 15-17, the interpolator has doubled the description of the Judgment, thereby quite clumsily making the Son of Man identical with an angel, etc. etc. Especially the last chapters have been confused, and Charles takes it upon himself to re-establish the original order by having recourse to the method of philology and of rythmic analysis.

E. Lohmeyer and P. Allo strictly defend the absolute literary unity of the Apocalypse. According to Allo, those authors who speak of a compilation from various sources, have not been able "to sense the almost undefinable power" of John's symbolism (p. CLXXVIII). John's practice of "framing" a future scene in his own words, and of "waves," whereby he presents the same event under several different aspects, should suffice to explain the repetitions (cf. the explanation of these practices on pp. LXXVIII-XCVI). The visions at the base of the Apocalypse are real, although they may be either imaginative or intellectual. The ingenious structure of the Book is hardly valid reason for impugning the authenticity of the ecstatic experience which the author says he has been allowed to have. Nevertheless, it is also evident that John has put forth an intense effort in the task of literary elaboration, using these same apocalyptic fragments written by other authors. The only case, however, in which Allo considers this likely, is 14: 14-20, the scene of the harvest and vintage.

Standing on his basic premise that the Apocalypse is a single work, P. Allo proceeds to determine its general structure. First of all, there are two main sections, *that which exists now* (the letter to the seven churches of Asia), and *that which is to come later* (all the following, from chapter 4 to chapter 21). This latter section which alone is really prophetic, is again divided into two parts. The former of these goes from the opening in heaven with the book with the seven seals (chapters 6-7) and the earthly execution of the divine decrees (the septet of the trumpets, chapters 8-11). Chapter 10 is an interlude, after which the second prophetic part comes in, dealing with the decrees of the little book (11: 19 - 21: 8) and containing the introductory visions, in which the opposing forces are presented (the Woman and the Dragon: chapter 12); the two Beasts and the Lamb with his 144,000 virgins (13; 14: 1-5); the preparation for the battle, which corresponds to the septet of the seals (14: 6-20),

and finally the defeat of Christ's enemies in the reverse order
of their appearance; the septet of the bowls corresponding
to that of the trumpets (chapters 15-16); the destruction of
Babylon and of the Beasts (chapters 17-19); the temporary
imprisonment of Satan, the reign of 1000 years; the last
attack and the eventual definitive defeat of Satan (20: 1-10).
This second part ends with the resurrection of the dead, the
general judgment of all mankind, the appearance of the new
heaven and the new earth (20: 11 - 21: 8). The following
section, containing the lengthy description of the heavenly
Jerusalem, spouse of the Lamb (21: 9 - 22: 5) is, in the eyes
of Allo, a separate section, the third and final section of the
Apocalypse.

    Lohmeyer sees the structure of the Apocalypse as follows:
in chapter 14 is the peak of the book, with the Lamb on
Mt. Sion; all the preceding material refers to the world's
resistance to the Lamb and to the punishment which is to
befall it. After an introduction (chapters 4-5), comes the
properly apocalyptic section, comprising seven series and
seven visions. Lohmeyer finds himself constrained, however,
to resort to some rather arbitrary manipulations of the text,
in order to arrive at the seven visions which he wishes to see
in last of the seven sections. Hadorn also distinguishes seven
septets, each divided into seven parts, but his divisions are
entirely different from those of Lohmeyer.

    Loisy, like Allo, Lohmeyer and Hadorn, also recognize
the stylistic unity of the Apocalypse, and the existence of a
regular plan, which he considers to be as follows: the septets
of the letters, the seals, the trumpets and the bowls, are so
many stages of the eschatological drama, beginning with
the present state of the Christian communities, and looking
forward to the end of the present world and the inauguration
of a new one (p. 21). However, this very artificial structure

fails to account for the doublets and the interpolations. G. Baldensperger is with the same opinion (pp. 413-415).

A. Wikenhauser, who holds that the Apocalypse is nothing but a further elaboration of Jesus' eschatological discourse (Mk. 13 and parallel texts), offers a hypothesis which distinguishes (as does Jesus' discourse) three acts in the final drama: in the first act (5: 1 - 11: 14) are the events preliminary to the final battle between God and Satan (cf. in the Synoptic apocalypse, the "beginning of sorrows," Kr. 8); the second act shows the battle in progress between God and Satan (11: 15 - 20: 15; cf. the great tribulation of the Synoptic apocalypse): third act, the eternal Kingdom of God and the heavenly Jerusalem (21: 1 - 22: 5). E. Schick presents a similar structure in his commentary in the *Echter-Bibel*.

Neither A. Gelin, J. Bonsirven, nor Ch. Brütsch, have undertaken a profound study of the structure of the Apocalypse. M. E. Boismard, on the other hand, has plumbed the problem deeply. As we have indicated above (pp. 18-19), he is of the opinion that the Apocalypse is all the work of one and the same author, but he still has doubts about its internal coherence. He emphasizes, first of all, the unusual number of doublets, for example the 144,000 faithful whose foreheads are signed by the angel (7: 2-8) and the corresponding 144,000 who bear the name of God on their foreheads (14: 1-5). The parallelism is also evident between the seven sets of the trumpets (chapters 8-9) and of the bowls (chapter 16). There are two descriptions of the Beast with the seven beads of the ten horns, (13: 1-8; 17: 3, 8), and of the ideal Jerusalem of the future (21: 1-8; 21: 9 - 22: 5), as well as the two announcements of the fall of Babylon (14: 8 and 18: 2 - 3) etc., etc. Other inconsistencies are the descriptions, apparently given for the first time, of persons

and things already presented; for example, the Beast represents the Roman empire in chapter 13, and the Emperor Nero
in chapter 17. These indications have led Fr. Boismard to
conclude that the present Apocalypse is a combination of two
distinct works, originally independent and eventually joined
together. For Boismard's detailed explanation of the separation of the two original works, cf. the Apocalypse fascicule
of the *Bible de Jérusalem* (p. 12).

SPECIAL STUDIES

We might mention in passing, the fanciful works of P. L.
Couchoud, *L'Apocalypse*, 1922 and 1930. The 1922 work is
only a translation. That of 1930 maintains that the prophet
has produced his work in two successive versions.

In his article *Johannesapokalypse* (in RGG, 2nd edition
volume III, 1929, coll. 336-338), H. Windisch raises the
following objections against the unity of the Apocalypse:
the essentially Christian eschatology of the inaugural vision,
of the letters and with the conclusion of the Church, would
be very much different from the Old Testament Jewish
eschatology which characterizes the visions. The three series
of plagues, (seals, trumpets, bowls) must have been originally independent descriptions, since each of them leads
eventually to the final catastrophe and to ultimate salvation.
In chapter 10 the Seer receives a second apocalyptic book,
which seems to be an indication of a further addition. The
Babylonian seductress is a doublet of the first Beast. In fine,
Windisch concludes to an original fundamental work, which
was later enlarged by the author himself, or by another
(the original apocalypse contained, he says, only the introductory vision, the letters, the septet of the seals and the
conclusion).

In his book *The Book of Revelation* (Cambridge, 1923,) J. W. Oman sees the present order of the Apocalypse as due to an accidental re-arrangement of pages, some of which were not intended to be included in the work, thereby causing the interpolation of extraneous material. In his attempt to reconstruct the original, Oman comes up with such hypotheses as the following: 3: 22 is followed by 10: 1 - 14: 5; and 22: 6-8a is additional but should be placed after 10: 10; 11: 14-19 should be deleted, etc., etc. Oman has presented his theory, somwhat revised, in *The Text of Revelation* (Cambridge, 1928).

Gaechter has published in *Theological Studies* a series of articles on the literary composition of Apocalypse: *Semitic literary forms in the Apocalypse and their import* (VIII, 4, 1947, p. 547-573); *The Role of Memory in the Making of the Apocalypse* (IX, 3, 1948, pp. 419-452); *The Original Sequence of Apocalypse 20 - 22* (X, 4, 1949, pp. 483-521). The net conclusion to be drawn from these articles is that the original order of the Apocalypse has been subjected to transposition, omissions, and additions. He explains that John had recounted his visions orally to a disciple, who recorded them from memory, forgetting some details and injecting some modifications.

In his article *L'Apocalypse de saint Jean devant la critique moderne* (NRT, 1924, pp. 513-525; 596-618), J. Levie presents his view that there is in the Apocalypse a strictcly chronological succession of seven septets; in addition to the septets of the letters, seals, the trumpets, and the bowls, there are also seven signs, (12: 1 - 14: 4), seven kinds of persons who rejoice at the destruction of Babylon (17: 1 - 19: 3), seven scenes relating to the wedding feast of the Lamb, of which the last is eternal blessedness (19: 4;

22: 5). The seventh moment is not so much an incident, as rather, the beginning of a new septet. (p. 603.)

Similar to P. Levie's study is that of R. Loenertz, *Plan et division de l'Apocalypse* in *Angelicum* 18 (1941) pp. 336-356. According to Loenertz, the Apocalypse is made up of seven septets, each preceded by an introductory section. Furthermore, the seventh member of each of the six last septets is a résumé of the foregoing: the last seal goes from 11: 15 to 22: 5; the seventh sign from 15: 1 to 22: 5; the seventh bowl from 16: 17 to 22: 5, etc.

In his article on the Apocalypse in *Catholicisme* (Tome I. coll. 689-693), L. Vaganay also distinguishes seven septets, but without placing any chronological connection between them. Msgr. Chalve is much more systematic in his treatment in *L'Apocalypse, traduction et présentation nouvelle,* (Marseille, 1953). According to his study, the seven septets contain each other, in such a way that the last member of each septet includes the following septet. J. W. Bowmann (*The Revelation to John, Its Dramatic Structure and Message,* in *Interpretation,* 1955, pp. 436-453), sees the Apocalypse as a drama in seven acts, each of which is divided into seven scenes. Bowmann insists that proper appreciation of this dramatic structure is essential for full understanding of the message of the book.

The article of A. Merk, *De compositione Apocalypsis* (VD 1928, pp. 211-218), contains only some brief comments. Father Merk shows himself to be favorable to the recapitulation theory, and rejects any suggestions of chronological progression in the Apocalypse, even within the septets.

J. Turmel's work *L'Apocalypse,* (Paris, 1938) emphasizes mainly the paradoxical thesis that the Apocalypse is a Jewish work of the time of Hadrian, originally written in Hebrew, then put into Greek, and eventually Christianized.

STRUCTURE OF THE APOCALYPSE

La Clé de l'Apocalypse, by A. Olivier, (Paris, 1938) sees in the Apocalypse a most extraordinary arrangement of literary elements: six sections of approximately equal length, containing 60 pericopes, each of which is divided in its turn into verses of three stanzas, giving a total of 600 stanzas (6 plus 60 plus 600 equals 666, cf. 13: 18). Olivier goes on to study what he calls the "grammatical elements," devising here too the most arbitrary systems imaginable. Each part contains 888 grammatical elements, which number, according to the Sybilline Oracles (1: 328-330), is the gematric number of the name of Jesus (I equals 10; ē equals 8; s equals 200, o equals 70; y equals 400; s equals 200).

The highly unfavorable judgment of the critics has not discouraged Olivier from producing more studies. These are: *La strophe sacrèe en saint Jean*, Paris, 1939, *Les premières strophes de l'Apocalypse*, Paris, 1947; *L'Apocalypse et ses enseignements, L'Introduction générale, Commentaire des messages aux Eglises*, Paris, 1954; *Apocalypse I, Premiére Partie (L-III), texte et traduction avec annexe (La composition strophique dans les Gèorgiques de Virgile)*, Paris, 1954.

Also worthy of mention are: R. R. Brewer, *The influence of Greek Drama upon the Apocalypse*, in ATR, 18 (1936), pp. 74-92; D. F. Montagnini, *Apocalisse 4: 1 - 22: 5; L'Ordine nel Caos*, in Riv. B, 1957, p. 180-196. According to these, the Apocalypse is composed of seven basically equal septets, because the scientific mind delights in tracing patterns in terms of concentric circles. Cf. also G. Bornkamm, *Die Komposition der apokalyptischen Visionen in der Offenbarung Johannis, Studien zu Antike und Urchristentum. Gesammelte Aufsätze*, Band II, Munich, 1959, pp. 204-222.

H. Hubert in *L'architecture des lettres aux sept èglises*, in R. B. 1950, pp. 349-353, sees the churches divided into

guilty (the odd numbers, 1, 3, 5, 7), and innocent (the even
numbers, 2, 4, 6): The guilt continues to increase (Laodicea,
the last, is accused most strongly of all) as also does the
holiness (Philadelphia is the holiest of the innocent).

CONCLUSION

In general, modern exegetes are less and less favorable
to arbitrary hypotheses which would reduce the Apocalypse
to a formless collection of various fragments. The unity of
thought and of style compel us to see the work as a complete whole.

Still, without prejudice to the ecstatic experience with
which it begins (Cf. C. Schneider *Die Erlebnisechtheit der
Apokalypse des Johannes,* Leipzig, 1930), the work is more
than a mere recounting of several visions. Rather, it is the
end product of a process of reflection and composition which
has had recourse to already existing elements. We are correct,
therefore, in speaking of a *pre-history* of the text, and along
this line we owe the profoundest gratitude to the pains-
taking efforts of Charles and of Fr. Boismard, and to their
careful attention of the minutest details of the text.

We might speak of successive redactions, beginning with
a primitive nucleus. There are, then, two successive Apocalypses and a second beginning at Chapter 12, which fact
we need to keep in mind throughout our study of the Book.
Swete says (*The Apocalypse of St. John,* p. XL) that if all
our MSS of the Apocalypse were to end at 11: 19, and the
following chapters were to be irretrievably lost, they would
probably not even be missed, since chapters 4-11 form in
themselves a concrete work, which could not have been
composed at the same time as the following chapters.

Furthermore, it seems correct to speak of the author's

making use of pre-existing documents; for example, in Chapter 11 and in the eschatological picture of 14: 14-20 (Cf. Allo pp. 242-243) etc. The important thing is, however, not to be so concerned with what meaning these fragments may have had at one time, but rather, with what meaning they have in the author's plan for the present context of the Apocalypse.

Even though he may have taken his inspiration from the various Jewish Apocalypses, John's work is, from beginning to end, a Christian book. Any attempt to delineate the individual Jewish sources seems to be doomed to frustration. John has made all his material entirely his own, and had conferred in it a uniquely Christological character. H. Windisch (R. G. G. Vol. III, cols. 337-338), says that the revelation of St. John could well be called the revelation of the Lamb. The opening and reading of the sealed book is the work of the Lamb; the anger shown at the calamities and at the (historical) judgments is that of the Lamb; it is against the Lamb that the Dragon enters into combat: God's victory is the Lamb's, and the eschatological salvation is described as the marriage in the feast of the Lamb.

True enough there are irregularities in the present order of the Apocalypse text. But these do not seem to us to be weighty enough to justify such attempts at literary dissection as have been undertaken, and which derive no support at all from the manuscript tradition. The impression of disorder and confusion which the text often conveys, can be due not only to the variety of the author's sources, but also to the fact that he has had recourse to such different literary forms as the epistolary form, which appears at the beginning, along with a salutation similar to those which we find at the beginning of most of the letters of the Pauline Corpus (cf. Apoc. 1: 4-5); the prophetic-apocalyptic form, which

predominates, beginning with Chapter 4, but which is anticipated from the beginning. Immediately after he has written
his introduction in the epistolary form, the author has recourse to the great inaugural vision of Christ glorified, very
much in the style of the ancient prophets.

We should have in mind that the apparent lack of coherence is almost a law of the apocalyptic style. E. F. Scott goes
so far as to say that a perfectly logical apocalypse would be
nothing short of a contradiction in terms (*The Book of Revelation*, p. 26)! The visions, real or not, which are described
here, are necessarily obscure and complicated (Cf. Ezechiel,
whose style is the remote ancestor of this literary genre),
insofar as the reader is led constantly from earth to heaven
and back again. The Seer seeks to translate the ideas which
God grants him by the use of symbols and other details,
such as colors, numbers, etc. without being concerned with
the specific effect of these images on his readers. This antho-
logical style, which is characteristic of the apocalyptic literature in general, and of St. John's Apocalypse in particular,
adds to the obscurity of the text. Often the author brings
about, without even intending to do so, an unexpected
synthesis of apparently disparate Old Testament elements,
superimposing on them his specifically Christian coloring.

By and large, the peculiarities of the Apocalypse are not
as great as they are often said to be. The greatest of these is
the apparently frequent recurrence of doublets. However,
even many of these are not what they may seem to be at
first glance. We shall show below, for example, that the
septet of the bowls is not at all a repetition of the trumpet
septet; for that matter, neither are the two accounts of the
fall of Satan entirely equal (12: 9-12; 20: 2-3), nor are the
144,000 men signed by the angel the same as the 144,000
virgins who surround the Lamb on Mount Sion.

We are willing to make our own the remark of H. B. Swete, who remains today, as one of the best commentators of the Apocalypse:

"Such a list of apparent inconsistencies is formidable, as long as no one takes the trouble to subject it to close examination. Once this work is undertaken, however, the objections lose much of their weight. The elements, for example, which seem to indicate a plurality of authors, for the most part, can be explained in other ways, such as being due to the author's plan or to the exigencies of the literary style which he has adopted" (*The Apocalypse of St. John*, London, 1909, p. LII).

We would add that these problems are often no more than apparent. These inconsistencies, often superficial, really invite us, we think, to undertake a deeper, more penetrating exegesis. This approach, we feel, is preferable to the facile formulation of arbitrary literary laws, such as Allo has undertaken to do, only to avoid real difficulties.

As for the question of language, the letters at the beginning of the Apocalypse are written in a better style of Greek, than is the remainder of the book. It uses more delicate nuances, and chooses its particles carefully. Of course, the perspective here is different too, as we shall have occasion to point out below, but this hardly justifies a hypothesis of a separate source, although these letters may not have been written quite at the same time as the rest of the book.

It seems prudent to study the structure of the Apocalypse according to the text itself, as it is, separating insofar as is possible the problem of the literary composition from that of interpretation. Of course, it is no less than impossible to separate these aspects completely, but they can nevertheless be studied apart one from the other. The Apocalypse author describes four septets, those of the letters, the seals, the trumpets, and the bowls. It seems to us to be completely arbitrary to speak of seven septets, or to force a connection among all these septets that is greater than the text indicates.

We hold most of the views of Swete and Allo regarding the structure of the Apocalypse. The letters are clearly separate from the prophetic part, although we shall see below that these two parts are related. The prophetic part itself is divided into two large sections, each of which reaches its fulfillment. In the former section (4: 1 - 11: 19), the septet of the seals is the heavenly preparation for the septet of the trumpets. In the second prophetic section, (12: 1 to the end), the scenes of 14: 6-20 are the heavenly prelude to the septet of the bowls.

CHAPTER III

INTERPRETATION OF THE APOCALYPSE

COMMENTARIES

A. THE LETTERS (CHAPTERS 2-3).

The common opinion used to be that chapters two and three of the Apocalypse were a reproduction of real letters, which had been sent to each of the communities along with the body of the book. Spitta held this in *Offenbarung des Johannes*, (Halle, 1889). Charles' opinion is a little different (*The Revelation of St. John*, I, p. XCLV and pp. 43-46); according to him the seven letters, which make no allusion at all (except 3: 10) to either the cult of the emperor or to the prospect of a real persecution, are anterior to the rest of the book. Thus, they were sent by St. John to the Churches about the end of the time of Vespasian, but were later retouched by the author himself, and incorporated into his great revelation, written during the reign of Domitian.

More and more writers nowadays (Allo, Loisy, Bonsirven, Brütsch, Cerfaux-Cambier), agree that the letters are inseparable from the whole of the Apocalypse, because of the many verbal and conceptual similarities which link them to the following chapters. The fact that the letters are symmetrically composed in themselves, and that "in each of them the Spirit addresses himself," not to one single Church, but to "the churches" (cf. 2: 7, and parallel passages), indicates that they are closely related, and never existed independently.

On the other hand, however, commentators are reluctant to reduce them to a pure fiction, as does Lohmeyer. The many allusions which they contain indicate that John was familiar with the conditions existing in each of the Churches, such as the struggle against the false prophets at Ephesus (2: 2), the action of the Nicolaites at Ephesus, Pergamum, and probably also at Thyatira (2: 6, 14-15, 20-23); the martyrdom of Antipas at Pergamum (2: 13) is the hope for the conversion of the Jews at Philadelphia (if this is the meaning of 3: 8-9). Furthermore, the choice of images is dictated, according to most commentators, by the desire to make recognizable allusions to the monuments, the history, or to current practices in each of the seven cities.

There is considerable disagreement about the exact meaning of the eschatological promises made to the one who overcomes (2: 7, 11, 17, 26-27; 3: 5, 12, 21). Some, such as Gelin, Loisy, Boismard, see them as referring exclusively to the future life. Others (Allo, Bonsirven) are aware that, in Johannine thought, eternal life begins here on earth. Thus they think that these promises are directed at the same time to the life of Christians as it is here on earth.

There are few commentators who still pursue the question whether, over and above the pastoral content, the letters also have some sort of prophetic meaning, such as would make of them an anticipated description of the future destiny of the Church, in seven separate stages, between Pentecost and the Parousia. According to J. du Plessis, e. gr., Ephesus (*EPHIEMI*, to send) refers to the Church of the

Apostles; Smyrna, (the City of Myrrh), to the Church of the martyrs; Pergamum (City of Parchment), to the churches of the Fathers, etc.

B. CHAPTERS 4-22.

Now we can turn to the second principal part of the Apocalypse (Ch. 4 to the end), the part which is more properly prophetic. In this part, Allo distinguishes two clearly separate sections. The first of these (the septets of the seals and the trumpets), describes the execution of the decrees contained in the book of the seven seals, and deals with the judgments of God upon the world, after the Ascension of the Lamb that has been slain (Chapter 5), up to the last judgment, at the sound of the last trumpet (11: 14-18). Thus the future of the entire world is the object of the author's view, especially the future of the profane world.

The second prophetic section, beginning with Chapter 12, includes the predictions which the angel of Chapter 10 has instructed John to deliver. As does the first section, this one also views all of human history, but specifically from the viewpoint of the Church, and of the struggles which it must carry on now against the Roman empire, and which it will have to carry on until the Parousia.

The reign of 1000 years of Chapter 20 is related to the entire earthly phase of the Kingdom of God, which has been inaugurated by the exaltation of Christ. Thus it does not follow chronologically upon the plagues of the trumpets and of the bowls, but rather is contemporary to these events.

This interpretation offered by Allo, is very close to that of Bonsirven. L. Cerfaux and J. Cambier maintain positions similar to it. After the first prophetic section, which is modeled upon the style of the Jewish Apocalypses and that of the first Christian Apocalypses, the second section is designed to offer a revelation of the future of the Church and of the Roman empire. As for the Millenium, it is conceived here according to the manner of A. Wikenhauser, i.e., the resurrection which characterizes it is no more than the literary expression of the reward given to the martyrs. Thus the reign of 1000 years and the time of the persecuted Church are contemporary. Unlike Allo, (who sees the Church as simultaneously militant and triumphant), these authors see these last chapters (as 21: 9 - 22: 5) as applying only to the Jerusalem of the end - time.

Most authors now are opposed to the theory of recapitulation, and admit a more or less rigorous chronological succession in the Apocalypse. They see in the Millenium a definite stage of history (thus Charles, Baldensperger, Wikenhauser, Loisy, Boismard, Levie). The atemproal exegesis of the kind defended by Lohmeyer is generally rejected on the grounds of its being out of conformity with the New Testament revelation (cf. on this point O. Cullmann, *Christ et le Temps*, Neuchâtel - Paris, 1947, especially pp. 46-47).

Like Allo, Gelin generally accepts the Augustinian view of the Millenium. Otherwise, however, he inclines to an historical exegesis, like that of Renan. Thus there must be some sort of chronological succession. Each of the plagues in the septets of the trumpets and of the bowls is to be interpreted historically, insofar as possible. According to this fundamental supposition, the first horseman is an allusion to the victory of the Parthian king Vologes over the Roman legions in the year 62; the second horseman is a reference to the events of 69, when Otho, Galba, Vitellius and Vespasian brought about a confrontation of the legions of the Rhineland, of Gaul, Greece and Asia; the third horseman suggests the famines suffered throughout the Roman empire in the second half of the first century; the fourth horseman thus is an allusion to the epidemics of 65 described by Tacitus (Annals XVI: 13) etc., etc. Chapter 11, a Jewish document adopted by St. John, would be thus a reference to the Jewish War, e. gr., the measuring of the Temple, would be nothing other than the preservation of the holy places, which were not destroyed until the end of the siege of Jerusalem; the two witnesses would be two Christian prophets of the years 68-70. Still in all, after the description of Domitian's rabid persecution, (Chapter 13), beginning with the septet of the bowls, the prophetic perspective cedes to the historical view; "from here on John looks to an indistinct future."

SPECIAL STUDIES

A. THE LETTERS (CHAPTERS 2 - 3)

Against Allo, E. Tobac (*Notes sur les trois premiers chapitres de l'Apocalypse,* in Museion, 39 (1926) pp. 345-367) thinks that the promises of the letters of the Apocalypse all have an eschatological meaning, which demonstrates the unravelling of the same themes as those of chapters 19-22; these are nothing but various ways of describing the same eternal glory which is to follow upon the final triumph of the Church. A. Skrinjar (*Praemia in Apoc. 2 et 3 victoriae proposita,* V.D. 1933, pp. 182-186; 232-239; 277-280; 295-301; 333-340) is less sure, but is close to the position of Allo. A. Olivier (*Commentaire des Messages aux Eglises,* p. 57), proposes to distinguish in the promises of the letters "a regular progression, beginning with the reception of grace, the fruit of the tree of life of the Ephesians, and leading to union with God, consummated in heaven before God's heavenly throne by the Laodiceans." E. Stauffer (*Christus und die*

Caesaren, Hamburg, 1952, p. 198) offers an attractive hypothesis of a close relationship between the style of the Apocalypse letters on the one hand, and the edicts of Domitian,
and of the great kings of Asia on the other. The heavenly
Emperor is the only real Master of history; he sends his
ambassadors to carry his messages to the churches which
fight for Him on earth.

L. Poirier offers an interesting hypothesis in his doctoral
thesis, *Les sept Églises ou le premier septénaire prophétique
de l'Apocalypse,* (Montreal, 1943). The subtitle of this work
explains that it is designed to show that these letters to the
seven churches have a prophetic character and have a view
of the universal Church of all times. He seeks to prove his
point by the number seven applied to the churches, the
rhythmic order of the text, the connection which links the
first septet to the future septets, and finally by the succession
of the promises. These promises, addressed not to individuals,
but to the new people of God, reproduce the successive
stages of the old Covenant (paradise, fall, captivity in Egypt,
Exodus, reigns of David and Solomon, etc.) and thus foretell, in general outline, the seven ages of the history of the
Church.

On the letters of the Apocalypse cf. F. Hoyos, *La carta
comun a las siete iglésias, Iniciacion a la parte parénética
del Apoc.,* in Rev B 18 (1956), p. 82-90; pp. 135-141; 198-203;
19 (1957), p. 18-22; *Los rasgos comunes de las siete cartas,*
ibid. 19 (1957), p. 82-86; *La fidelidad en el combate y el
premio,* 20 (1958), p. 73-77; 127-133; 190-193; I. Schuster,
La Chiesa e le sette chiese apocalittiche, in *Scuola Cattolica,*
81 (1953), p. 217-223; A. George, *Un appel a la fidelité,*
in BV Chr. 15 (1956), p. 80-86; H. Martin, *The Seven Letters,*
Philadelphia, 1956.

The following monographs are dedicated to the study of

particular points: Per Janzon, *Die Nikolaiten im Neuen Testament und der frühen Kirche,* in *Svensk Exegetisk Arsbok,* 1956, p. 82-108; A. Ehrhardt, *Das Sendschreiben nach Laodizea,* in EvTh. 1957, p. 431-445; M.J.S. Rudwick and E.M.B. Green, *The Laodicean Luckewarmers,* in ExpT 1958, p. 176-178; A. Jankowski, *Manna Absconditum* (*Apoc.* 2, 17) *quonam sensu ad Eucharistiam referatur,* in *Collectanea Theologica,* 29, 1958, p. 3-9.

B. CHAPTERS 4-22.

We might mention briefly here the study of Marc del Medico, *Les predictions de l'Apocalypse,* (Paris, 1922), who holds that chapter 12 of the Apocalypse recounts the earthly birth of Christ, with all the preceding material (beginning with chapter 4) dealing with the Old Testament.

Boll (followed partly by Loisy) held that the Apocalypse seeks not so much to describe visions which the author has really lived, as rather to express Christian hope of the use of symbols borrowed from Hellenistic cosmology and astrology, which in their turn are of Babylonian origin. Thus the plague of the trumpets and the bowls is based on a picture of cosmological anthropology found in chapter 6 of Hippocrates' *PERI HEBDOMADŌN* and chapter 30 of the Slavonic Henoch (Adam created from the seven parts of the universe and endowed with seven essences). The basic idea here is that the microcosm and macrocosm (man) are divided into seven parts, which balance each other perfectly. J. Freundorfer has produced an important work refuting these positions, *Die Apokalypse des Apostels Johannes und die hellenistische Kosmologie und Astrologie,* (Freiburg i. B., 1929). In it Freundorfer shows in particular that the Hellenistic calendars upon which Boll bases his thesis were not as precise as Boll seems to presume they were. The year of the Virgo, e.g., (related to the second horseman), was not necessarily a war year; neither was the year of the Scales (cf. the 3rd horseman) a year of famine, nor was the year of Scorpio (4th horseman) one of sickness.

In his thesis *L'Antechrist et l'opposition au Royaume Messianique dans l'Ancien et le Nouveau Testament*, (Gembloux–Paris, 1932), B. Rigaux has a long section dedicated to the Apocalypse (pp. 318-387). According to this thesis, the Apocalypse is to be interpreted according to the theory of recapitulation. The first of the two Beasts, which becomes incarnate in the Roman empire at a precisely given moment in history, is especially a symbol of all the anti-Christian forces of humanity. The second Beast represents the powers of persuasion hostile to Christianity. Thus the section is not at all a prophecy of the syncretism of the second and third centuries (against Allo).

R. Schütz (*Die Offenbarung des Johannes und Kaiser Domitian*, Göttingen, 1933), sees the first Beast as Titus and the second as Domitian. He seems inclined to stress the verbal similarities between the titles attributed to Christ in the Apocalypse hymns, and those which Domitian attributed to himself; he arrives eventually at the conclusion that the number of the Beast in 13: 18 is not 666, but 616 (according to a variant supported by C and by St. Irenaeus), corresponding to an imperial seal of the 16th year of Domitian (DCXVI equals Domitian Caesar XVI). Then according to S. Minear, *The Wounded Beast*, in JBL 72 (1953), pp. 93-101, John, in speaking of the Beast as mortally wounded (13: 3, 12, 14), is not referring to any historical personage, but is availing himself rather of the terminology of the old traditions, in order to allude to Christ's victory on the cross.

P. Touilleux, in his book *L'Apocalypse et les cultes de*

Domitien et de Cybéle (Paris, 1935), clearly reacts against Allo's exegesis and recapitulation theory. Touilleux's opinion is that St. John has conformed his work to the fundamentally fictional character of the Jewish Apocalypses, in which the events of past and present are projected into the future as real predictions. Thus St. John's Apocalypse was composed in the time of Domitian, and is presented as a revelation received under Vespasian, about the year 68. Chapters 2 and 3 are allusions to the events of Vespasian's reign. The following chapters, 4 - 14: 7, describe in Apocalyptic style, and under the form of prophetic oracles, a series of calamities which are to occur between 68 - 95 (the real time in which the work was written). The author of this study emphasizes the perfect way in which the vision of the two Beasts in chapter 13 is adapted to the circumstances of Domitian's reign, in which the predominant Cybele cult was closely allied in Asia Minor to that of the Emperor. On these supposed relationships between the Apocalypse and the Cybele cult, cf. the studies of L. Cerfaux in ETL, 13, 1936, pp. 527ff and of J. de Fraine, in SDB, cols. 111-113.

S. Giet has offered a study based on a reading of the works of Josephus Flavius, and suggesting a possible connection between this author and the Apocalypse, in *L'Apocalypse et l'Histoire* (Paris, 1957). He undertakes a closely detailed comparison between Apoc. 8: 13 - 11: 19, and the various phases of the Jewish War under Vespasian, as it is narrated by Josephus. The characteristics of the first woe (9: 1-12) suggest the troubles which plagued Palestine under the rule of Florus. The second woe (9: 13-21), characterized by four angels of Judgment, who come from the Euphrates, is similar to the invasion and pillaging realized under Cestius, who brought with him four contingents of troops, part of them from the Euphrates region. The third woe, which is not really described (11: 14), seems to refer to the final destruction of the Temple, which is balanced (11: 19) by one opening of the heavenly sanctuary. Giet offers other interesting parallels between Josephus and these elements of the Apocalypse, insisting that the Apocalypse could not be atemporal, since so many historical allusions could hardly be pure accident.

This last idea was a favorite of Fr. Huby, and was the basis of a long-protracted dispute between him and Father Féret. In *Apocalypse et Histoire* (*Construire*, XV, 1944, pp. 80-100), Fr. Huby notes two tendencies among Apocalypse commentators: in the one is that of those who look only at Roman history, in the period from Nero to Domitian; the others lift the Apocalypse above contemporary history, thereby broadening its meaning considerably. Father Huby prefers the former of these two methods. In *Apocalypse, Histoire et Eschatologie Chrétienne* (*Dieu Vivant*, no. 2, 1945, pp. 117-144), Father Féret maintains the opposite, saying that the symbols of the Apocalypse have a definitely prophetic value, and look to the future without giving a detailed or concrete prediction of it. Father Huby replies to this in *Autour de l'Apocalypse* (*Dieu Vivant* no. 5, 1946, pp. 121-130). In his article Father Huby offers some new considerations, e.gr., that it is useless to find in the Apocalypse any clear view of the Church's development, because the prophecy is not really any kind of foreseeing of future history, such as would be limited to the measure of time. Similar views are at the base of the work by J. Cambier, *Les images de l'Ancien Testament dans l'Apocalypse*, in NRT, 1955, pp. 113-122. In this article Father Cambier warns against the tendency to place too much historical value in the images which the Apocalypse author has borrowed in large measure from the Old Testament.

On the imagery of the Apocalypse, cf. also K. L. Schmidt, *Die Bildersprache in der Johannesapokalypse*, in Th Lit Z, 1947, pp. 161-177; Schmidt maintains here that the images of the Apocalypse often appear to be incoherent precisely because they are designed to emphasize unspeakable supernatural realities: Christ as lion and lamb in 5: 5-6; bitter and sweet in 10: 9; the voice of many waters (Judgment), and the harpers playing on their harps in 14: 2; the sea of glass and fire in 15: 2; the fanciful description of the heavenly Jerusalem as a cube (symbol of perfect harmony) in 21: 16; the locusts of Chapter 9, as an indication of the ugliness of the lower world, etc. A. Farrer, holds (*A Rebirth of Images, The Making of St. John's Apocalypse*, London, 1949), that the Apocalypse visions are based on an adaption of the images used on the occasion of Jewish feasts: Tabernacles; Dedication; Passover; Pentecost (cf. below on the liturgical character of the Apocalypse). On this point cf. also C. Clemen, *Visionen und Bilder in der Offenbarung Johannis*, Th. St. Kr. 107, 1936, p. 236-265; W. Forster, *Die Bilder in Offenbarung* 12 *f. und* 17 *f.*, *Neutestamentliche Forschungen*, Th. St. Kr., 104, 1932, p. 279-310.

In the *Revue Ecclésiastique de Liége*, 1931, H. Rongy offered several fine brief articles on the interpretation of the Apocalypse; cf. *Le premier septénaire de l'Apocalypse ou le livre aux sept sceaux* (p. 3-13); *Rome ou le chapitre* 17 *de l'Apocalypse* (31-37); *L'application de l'Apocalypse a l'histoire universelle de l'Eglise* 92-95; *L'Explication eschatologique de l'Apocalypse* (158-165); *L'application de l'Apocalypse à l'Église primitive* (220-224). Cf. Also K. Schmidt, *Aus der Johannes - Apokalypse, letzten Buch der Bibel*, Basel, 1946; J. Rohmer, *L'Apocalypse et le sens chrétien de l'histoire*, RevScR, 26 (1952), pp. 265-270; F. Spadafora, *L'Apocalisse*, RivB, 2, 1954, pp. 299-309. In *Table Ronde* (no. 110,

Fevrier, 1957), J. Steinmann (*Remarques sur l'Apocalypse,* p. 48-53), defends the paradoxical thesis that the Apocalypse is interested only in the atemporal victory of the Lamb and his Spouse, without being opposed to an evolutionary view of the world. In the same issue of the *Table Ronde,* A. Hammann states exactly the opposite (pp. 54-62), i.e., that the Apocalypse is definitely a prophecy of the history of salvation.

We might mention also the following works: E. S. Jenkins, *The Time of the End,* 1939; H. S. Bellamy, *The Book of Revelation in History,* London, 1942; H. Kuhaupt, *Der neue Himmel und die neue Erde,* 1947; L. Herrmann, *L'Apocalypse johannique et l'histoire romaine,* Latomus 7 (1948), p. 23-46; G. Rudberg, *Apocalypse and the Enncade,* Conject. Neot. 12, 1948; Chr. H. W. Brekelmans, *Een nieuwe theorie over de Apoc.,* Stud. Theol. III 1951.

Conclusion

A. THE LETTERS

It seems correct to conclude that the letters of the Apocalypse never existed independently. They are not a pure fiction however, because they have in view some concrete circumstances of the condition of the Churches of Asia Minor. However, it seems furthermore that we should place more emphasis than is usually done, on their being oracles; it is not John, strictly speaking, who speaks to the churches, but it is Christ who comes as a sort of inspector, examining them closely, and exhorting them in His Spirit. Much more than the epistles of the properly so-called epistolary corpus of the New Testament, these letters are a recollection of the prophets of the Old Testament, especially of the seven oracles at the beginning of the Book of Amos, although we must be careful to distinguish between the similarity of form and the great difference between the intentions of the respective authors: foretelling of divine punishment on the one hand, and, on the other, pastoral exhortations, and consoling promises, both rendered with an inimitable religious fervor (cf. L. Poirier, *L'Eglise dans l'Apocalypse*, Publication des Facultés S. J. de Montreal, 1962, pp. 129-142). The promises made to him who overcomes, regard especially the future life, but not at all in such a way that they cannot look for a beginning of their fulfillment here below (at least some of them).

There is another clear indication of the special character of these letters, i.e., the fact that they are written to the angels of the churches. A simple glance at the commentaries can suffice to show what a variety of explanations have been offered for this. Some see them as the guardian angels of the churches (Holtzmann; Baldensperger; Lilye; Boismard; Bonsirven); or as messenger angels, assigned to bring Christ's commands to the churches (Sickenberger), as personifications of the communities themselves (Bousset, Charles, Lohmeyer, Swete, Behm, Gelin), or as the leaders of the churches, i.e., as bishops or groups of presbyters (Strack-Billerbeck, Zahn, Hadorn) or, by Cerfaux and Cambier, as a messenger sent by the churches to the Apostolic author himself. Allo prefers a "Symbolism of many levels," whereby each of the angels is a symbolic representative of the spirit of one Church, insofar as it is incarnate in its head, the bishop. In any case, there is no reason at all to eliminate the meaning which the word "angel" has in the Apocalypse. True enough, it does seem somewhat strange that John should address himself to angels, but then, this is certainly compatible with the apocalyptic literary form. In Daniel

(10: 13; 12: 1) angels are charged with the destruction of nations.

Should we see the letters as having a prophetic meaning? The arguments which some adduce from the text itself in this regard are not convincing, as we can judge from the variety of the hypotheses. Neither is there great probative force to be drawn from the exegesis of the Fathers or the medieval commentators, for the idea of a seven years' duration is no more a part of the faith now than are the fantastic interpretations which grew out of this supposition, when the tendency was so strong to find in the Apocalypse the seven ages of the Church. Still, there can be no doubt that to the eyes of the inspired author the seven churches are a representation of the universal Church and that the teachings which they contain are valid for the entire Church of every age.

B. CHAPTERS 4-22

1. *Methodology*

First of all we shall offer some general observation. Even with regard to this section of the Apocalypse, it hardly seems justifiable to resurrect any of the various versions of the theory of the seven ages of the world (system of history of the universe), which was popular chiefly during the Middle Ages. The best proof of the falsity of this theory is that it has to be changed in every age, in order to show that the period of calamity in which the commentator lives, can be the time immediately preceding the end of time. We do not think it is even possible to find in the Apocalypse any precise indication of the future of the Church, which would satisfy our curiosity.

Still in all, it is true that the Apocalypse author does have in his mind's eye some various important stages in the history of humanity. The real burden of the revelation is not so much the events in themselves (which for the most part are already past), or their real bearing on the inauguration of the Kingdom of God. The catastrophe of the destruction of the Temple in 70 is already over and done with (in our opinion, at least; cf. below), but John shows the meaning of this major event in the two septets of the seals and of the trumpets. The persecution of Christians by the emperors is already underway, but John undertakes to show what will be the eventual outcome.

At this point a comparison of the Apocalypse data with the Book of Daniel (7-12) brings welcome light. The final editing of Daniel dates from the time of Maccabean uprising (160 B. C.). Thus the description of events in the manner of a prophecy of what is to come in the future, is rather a return to the past, a review of the various empires, which the author shows in relation to the ultimate direction of God's plan, which is the final inauguration of the Day of the Lord and of the Kingdom of God. The future is not described in detail; rather, the author predicts in apocalyptic language that the era of persecution will come to an end and that God will have the last word over His enemies. The same perspective is characteristic of St. John's Apocalypse. In both books the reference to past history, whether proximate in John, or more remote, as in Daniel, serves as an example of what is to come. The author in each case is convinced of the future, and of the oneness of God's plan. Thus he frames his imagery in such a way that it is always directed toward the eschatological final event, which remains on the future historical horizon, to be realized as the end of

the present historical crisis which he experiences, and which
occasions his present writing.

We are greatly indebted to the many studies related to
the *zeitgeschichtlich* method, which was pioneered by Alcazar. According to this method, the Apocalypse is not atemporal, but rather, as we have seen, it fits into the series of
events contemporary to the author's writing, and is best
understood in the light of them. However, as A. Hammann
says, "the modern reader is not as well informed as the
reader with regard to the first century of the Christian era.
Thus there is considerable doubt with regard to the histor-
icity of many of the events recounted, and there is always
the danger of taking things out of their context, because of
an insufficient understanding of the literary form" (*La
Table Ronde,* February, 1957, p. 57). Thus, such allusions as
these are not as essential to the work, as Rénan's *Antéchrist*
would make them. The Apocalypse is intended, first and
foremost, to be a sort of Christian philosophy of history,
and a prediction of its ultimate outcome.

In our opinion, with the exception of the system of *the
history of the universe* as it was propounded by Joachim of
Flores and Nicholas of Lyre, all the various methods proposed for explaining the Apocalypse have something to
offer. Thus, the so-called *religionsgeschichtlich* method is not
the only one in which we see elements of good. The symbolism of John uses devices from the idea of the cosmos which
was common at the time; cf. V. Burch, *Anthropology and the
Apocalypse. An Interpretation of the Book of Revelation
in relation to the archaeology, folklore and religious literature and ritual of the near East,* 1939. Thus it is not at all
impossible that some mythical or astrological elements, which
had passed into general folklore, may have found their way
into the substrate of the Apocalypse imagery. However, this

is far from concluding that St. John's Apocalypse is nothing but a grandiose elaboration of pagan elements for the benefit of Christianity! This practice of looking for extra-biblical parallels must be undertaken with great caution, because of the temptation to exaggerate similarities. Fr. Allo's change in method is interesting in this regard; at first, he preferred to accept some of Boll's explanations, but later he dropped these in favor of the more critical investigations of the astrological theory undertaken by Freundorfer (cf. R. B. 1930 pp. 599-602). Instead of looking so much for extra-biblical parallels, it seems quite preferable to benefit from the work of the *traditionsgeschichtlich* school, and to consider the history of the traditions of which the Apocalypse author has availed himself, especially those traditions contained in the Scriptures themselves. It is certain that most of the images and themes which John uses are of a traditional character, and are found either in earlier Christian writings, or in the New Testament. Thus it seems erroneous either to look for too much historical character in any one of the symbols or images which the Apocalypse author has adopted, or to insist on looking for an explanation outside the Bible itself. Thus we should note that the dragon of 12: 4 has helpful parallels in Ex. 19: 4, Dt. 32: 11, and Is. 40: 31, without the necessity of invoking Boll's astrology (the *aquila* constellation), or the Mandaean themes of Lohmeyer (in which Miryai is pursued by the Jews, until Anosh comes to her aid in the form of a white eagle). The Apocalypse makes considerable use of numbers. The number three pertains to God; four, to the world; added together (seven), or multiplied (twelve), they express God's perfect action in the universe. The powers hostile to God, which can only fail in their attempts to thwart Him, are indicated by irregular numbers, e.gr., three and one-half, which is half of seven, or six as half of twelve, or seven minus one (as a symbol of limited or frustrated perfection). The Beast from out of the sea has seven heads, true enough, but this is because it dares to ape the power of God. This numerical language has parallels in contemporary Jewish apocalyptic, in the Old Testament, and in the pagan cults. However, as we said above, it seems preferable to us to look first of all for parallels in the biblical texts themselves, e.gr., the seven lamps of chapters 4-5 may be a recollection of the seven-branch candlestick; the seven thunders of 10: 3-4 recall Ps. 29, in which the voice of Jahweh as Judge of the universe echoes forth seven times. The forty two months of thirty days, which come to 1260 days or three and one-half years, can be explained from Daniel (7: 25; 9: 27; 12: 7). We could offer the hypothesis of a biblical origin for other cases as well, and in such cases the fact of a biblical parallelism would be more illuminating than we might expect. This seems to be the case also with regard to 8: 7 and 9: 15 (cf. below).

2. General Meaning of the Two Prophetic Sections

Given all this, we can now proceed with a brief, if superficial, analysis of the prophetic part of the Apocalypse. We shall begin with the less difficult, and pass from this to the more difficult, i.e., by beginning at the end, with the description of the heavenly Jerusalem. From there we shall pass on to the second prophetic section of the Apocalypse (12: 1 - 21: 8), and finally to the first (chapters 4-11), which seems to pose the most difficult problems of all.

We are inclined to favor the strictly eschatological interpretation of this description of the new Jerusalem (with most commentators, and against Allo). The data of 21: 24-27, which seem to interrupt this perspective, and to refer to the Church militant, refer to the Old Testament sources which the author has attempted to adapt to his purpose. This vision is the crowning point of the whole book; it shows the eternal dwelling of the elect, an unchangeable city (measured by God), perfect in itself (the image of the cube), and at the same time a temple, brightened by the glory of God and by the Lamb. The author has in mind the rivers of Ezechiel's earthly paradise, and also the Jewish pilgrims who go up to Jerusalem "to see the face of Jahweh." All these Old Testament preparations, especially the desire to see God, arrive here at a beautiful fulfillment; they also attest to the unity of God's plan, as it is clearly discernible in the unity of the Bible.

The general plan of the second prophetic section of the Apocalypse (12: 1 - 21: 8), has been well explained by Fr. Allo and by most commentators. The authors are almost unanimous (with the exception of a few, such as Sickenberger, Freundorfer, Lohmeyer, etc), in seeing that the historical background of this section is the persecution which the Roman emperors have unleashed against the Church. The Beast coming up out of the sea represents first of all the Roman empire as the persecutor coming from the West (recognizable to Palestinians as the sea), and typifies all totalitarian states which will presume to follow the example of the intolerant emperors. As for the second Beast, which comes up from the earth (Asia), and acts as a prophet, placing its power at the service of the former Beast, John undoubtedly sees this second Beast as the incarnation of all the pagan cults prevalent at the time favorable to the cult of the emperor. Thus all this part of the Apocalypse is basically a defiant reply to the emperors, who dare to demand worship for themselves. Such presumption can only be doomed to failure: pagan Rome can expect a fate no different from that of Babylon.

However, difficulties arise on every side when we try to go from these almost universally accepted generalities, to a more detailed explanation. For example, the authors favorable to the theory of *recapitulation* are mostly of the opinion that the septet of the bowls has in view exactly the same events as that of the seals, and merely describes them under a new form. We consider this exegesis unacceptable, especially because of the phrase in 15: 1, "The seven *last* plagues." One cannot favor a general recapitulation *a priori;* if the end of the Apocalypse really refers to the end of time in the strict sense, symbolized by the heavenly Jerusalem, then why should we not see the descriptions anterior to it, as leading progressively to this end, so that they follow each other according to a sort of chronological pattern?

This hypothesis seems to apply equally well to the explanation of the imprisonment of Satan and the reign of 1000 years in 20: 1-10. Allo and many others presume to suggest that these two facts, which are presented so neatly as following upon the destruction of pagan Rome, are nevertheless contemporary to the entire earthly phase of the Kingdom of God which begins with the Resurrection and Ascension. This seems to us to be impossible. As Fr. Levie says:-

> Such a system leads to a paradox and an impossibility; The reign of 1000 years, which presupposes that Satan is in confinement, and reduced to impotence (20: 3), could hardly have been desired by St. John as contemporary to the terrible crises unleashed by the release of Satan, who is allowed to be master of the earth for a time (12: 12) (NRT, 1924, p. 605).

As to just how we should understand this reign of 1000 years, we shall return later to this very complicated question (cf. below, chapter VII, on the Millenium).

Thus we come to the first prophetic section, chapters 4-11. The first point to be made is, that we cannot reject every idea of recapitulation, because the sound of the seventh trumpet coincides with the Resurrection of the dead and with the general judgment (cf. 11: 15-18). As we said above, there are, as it were, two complete apocalypses, one following the other, and both of which lead to the end of history. How can we explain this duplication? It would require more time and space than are available here, to develop our hypothesis completely. We must content ourselves here, therefore, with a few suggestions.

Against G. M. Camps (*Commentaire des Moines de Montserrat*, tome XXII p. 270), who denies, oddly enough, any direct connection between the sealed book and the plagues, the great majority of authors correctly think that the sealed book contains the announcement of the divine punishments described at the opening of each of the seals. Many also think, although against great opposition, that the first prophetic section of the Apocalypse differs from the second as a vague, general description differs from a precise and detailed account. This would lead to the strange result of having chapters 12 ff. give to the readers a burning interest in the meaning of the present events, while the preceding section would be completely detached from the contemporary situation. To us this is entirely unlikely. It seems to us to be just as correct to suspect the historicizing type of exegesis (Gelin, for example), which seeks to find in each symbolic figure of the Apocalypse an allusion to a concrete historical event, as it is to credit the author with an intention of addressing his fellow Christians in terms of the problems which they know

in their own lives. We shall presume this latter intention as
we pursue a backward glance, beginning with Chapter 11.

At the beginning of Chapter 11, John is given a reed like
to a rod, with which to measure the Temple of God, the
altar, and those who worship therein, but he must reject the
court which is outside the temple (TĒN AULĒN TĒN
EXŌTHEN EKBALE EXŌTHEN), because it has been
given to the nations which "will trample it underfoot for
42 months." Some commentators (Gelin, Giet) see here an
allusion to the Jerusalem Temple, which was destroyed toward the end of the first century. But how could the Apocalypse author limit himself to consider a purely material
preservation of the Jerusalem Temple, which he also knew
was not to last? Most exegetes see this passage (correctly)
as symbolic. Allo, Boismard and many others see it as dealing
with the Church in general, persecuted externally, and pre-
served intact internally. But then why must the scene be
limited to Jerusalem and the Temple? And is the end of
the verse an allusion to Lk. 21: 24, in which, in return for her
incredulity, Jerusalem "will be trodden down by the gentiles"? Would John have dared to apply to the persecuted
Church the oracle of Jesus?

The question becomes clearer, however, if we suppose
that the author, occupying himself from chapter 12 on with
the *relationship between the Church and pagan Rome*, here
has in view (as in the preceding chapters) *the relationship
between the Church and the chosen people*. Thus he gives
to his Church a structure which recalls that of the prophetic
books and of the Old Testament, first oracles against the
Jews, then oracles against the nations. Apoc. 11: 2 can be
related to Lk. 13: 25-28, in which the Jews of "outside"
knock on the door and seek to enter the banquet hall, but
find themselves "cast outside." Each of these two passages

contains the paradox of those who are outside, being cast outside. As Swete has noted (p. 133), John has in mind the final separation of the synagogue from the Church, which resulted from the catastrophe of 70, and refers here to the oracles of Ezechiel 40-48; Titus and his army have not destroyed the true Temple of God; it continues to stand, made up especially of Jews who have believed in Christ (the messianic remnant). The unbelieving Jews, who, because of the relationship between the Old Testament and the Gospel, could be compared to the exterior court of the Temple, are placed at the door. Cf. A. Feuillet, *Essai d'interprétation du chapitre 11 de l'Apocalypse*, in N.T.S. 4, April, 1958, pp. 183-200. M. Rissi defends this same exegesis with excellent arguments in *Zeit und Geschichte in der Offenbarung des Johannes*, Zürich, 1952, p. 123-133.

Next we turn to the septet of the trumpets, taken as a whole. The first point to be noted is that, although the bowls filled with the wrath of God upon the earth (16: 1), have no meaning other than one of punishment, still the symbol of trumpet sounds is not limited in the prophetic apocalyptic writings to a sense of wrath; in fact, trumpets are often used in the opposite way, to announce perfect harmony with God. Thus it is not at all accidental that the sound of the seventh trumpet is followed by the opening of the heavenly sanctuary and by the appearance of the ark of the covenant (11:19).

In 8: 7-12 the plagues of the four first trumpets work on the basis of thirds, and in 9: 15 there is no parallel to this element in the plagues of the bowls, which concern the pagan world. This difference can be explained in terms of the prophetic doctrine of the remnant (cf. the thirds in Ez. 5: 1 ff., and in Zacharia 13: 8-9). If we bear in mind also the similar allusions to Josephus' *Jewish War*, which Giet has discovered

in the detail of the plagues of the trumpets, and if we remember the connection between chapters 8-9, and chapter
11, which is the last of the septet of trumpets, located in
Jerusalem, we are virtually forced to conclude that the
plagues of the bowls are not at all a doublet of the trumpets,
because, whereas the bowls are related to the adorers and the
Beast, the trumpets are closely related to the divine judgment of the unbelieving Jews which was manifested in the
catastrophe of 70. And since the septet of the seals is a
heavenly preparation for that of the trumpets (cf. especially
Allo), it should have the same basic meaning. In fact, as
Charles has shown (*The Revelation of St. John* vol. I, pp.
158-159), it merely resumes and adapts the basic elements
of the Synoptic apocalypse. The 144,000 members of the 12
tribes of Israel, signed with the seal (7: 1-8) whom the author
contrasts with the innumerable multitude of gentile converts
(7: 9), refer to the remnant of Israel, and thus are distinct
from the 144,000 virgins assembled upon Mt. Sion (14: 1-5).

   That which, in the thought of Jesus, had an air of tragedy,
because it was to mark the end of centuries of religious
history, was not the judgment of all mankind at the end of
the world, but rather the fast approaching judgment of the
unbelieving Jews. J.A.T. Robinson (*Jesus and His Coming,*
London, 1957), recalls this basic truth well, although he
exaggerates in saying that, strictly speaking, Jesus never pre-
dicted His own Parousia. In any case, Robinson thinks
rightly that Mk. 13 and parallel texts refer to the Jews and
to Jerusalem; he is perhaps not wrong in thinking that the
apocalyptic coloring of this passage may have been added
(at least in part) by the primitive Christian community, who
read in it a foretelling of the Parousia. In the Apocalypse
4-11 we have a repetition of Mk. 13 and parallel texts, in
the double light of the inspiring influence of the Holy Spirit

and of the experience which the early Church had in the years following 70.

Certain authors (M. E. Boismard, J. Munck, *Petrus und Johannes in der Offenbarung Johannis*, Copenhagen, 1950) suspect that 11: 8 is a gloss, insofar as, beginning with chapter 12 the condemnation is always leveled at Rome and not at Jerusalem (cf. 16: 19; 17: 18; 18: 10, 16, 18, 19). If our exegesis is correct, the words of 11: 8, "where their Lord was also crucified" besides being fully supported by the manuscript tradition, are perfectly in place, insofar as, in the first prophetic section of the Apocalypse, the great city condemned by God is not Rome, but incredulous Jerusalem.

We are of the opinion that there is more than a passing significance to the placing of the last member of the septet of the trumpets in Jerusalem. Some have suggested that the two witnesses of 11: 3-13 are Peter and Paul, who were martyred in Rome (J. Mariana, *Scholia in Vetus et Novum Testamentum* Madrid, Paris, Antwerp, 1619, 1620, 1624; Boismard, also Munck in the work cited above). However, this hypothesis faces what seem to us to be insurmountable difficulties. How could we hope to harmonize the ancient tradition whereby the tombs of these two Apostles are venerated in Rome, with the resurrection and ascension of the two witnesses whose bodies are left unburied for three and one-half days in the streets of the great city? The two witnesses seem rather to be allegorical personages; they clearly suggest Moses and Elias; they are the incarnation of the ceaseless witness rendered in the Church to Christ by the Law (Moses) and the Prophet (Elias), in the face of a Judaism which remains obstinate in its refusal to believe. In 11: 13 a, the number of victims of the punishment (7000) corresponds to one-tenth of the city, showing that we are in Jerusalem, and not in Rome, which is much larger (cf. Allo, p. 155).

In 11: 13 b, the rest of the populace "give glory to the God of heaven"; Loisy notes (*L'Apocalypse*, p. 216), that this expression:

> *is not equivalent to being connected to the one God, and does not prove that the author has in mind a pagan city such as Rome* (this against Wellhausen).

Thus says Loisy, with many others, this is but a repetition of the prediction contained in Rom 11: 25-26, that the Jews will be converted at the end of time, when "the full number of the Gentiles "shall have entered the Church."

After even this brief survey, we remain convinced that some whole sections of the Apocalypse remain closed to us. We should give more attention than has been given so far to the relationship of the various septets to each other. It hardly seems likely that in a book as carefully planned as this one, these septets should be no more than accidental repetitions. We need also to look more deeply into the exact meaning of the Old Testament references (e.gr., the constant reference to Ezechiel in chapters 4-11), and to the pressing problems to which the Seer presumes to offer a salvation. Much, therefore, remains to be done.

CHAPTER IV

DOCTRINE OF THE APOCALYPSE

COMMENTARIES

Of all the recent commentators of the Apocalypse, Allo seems to be the one who has studied its doctrinal content most carefully. He maintains that it is incorrect to hold that the first generation of Christians lived every moment in expectation of the Parousia. Rather, the Christians of the primitive community were of the mind that the radical change had already taken place, because of the Incarnation and Redemption, and that Christ's final coming would not be the beginning of anything really new. This is the basic attitude of the New Testament authors, including the Apocalypse author, who teaches that Christ has already triumphed over the devil, and that the Christians are now assisting at the painful but guaranteed birth-pangs of the definitive era of final salvation. Bonsirven follows the same line of thought on this subject as Fr. Allo.

L. Cerfaux and J. Cambier take a slightly different view; while they do not deny the widespread expectation of the Parousia, which so many New Testament texts, including the Apocalypse, seem clearly to reflect; still they note (pp. 13 and 16) that this temporal proximity of the Parousia is merely a Semitic way of saying that the other world, that of pure spirit entirely different from the world of men, has begun, since the Resurrection, to enter directly into the world of men and time.

Most commentators hold that the Apocalypse is one of the most forceful witnesses to the belief in the second coming of Christ; cf. e.gr., Baldensperger, p. 440, note c.; Loisy, pp. 50-52; Gelin, pp. 665-666. Ch. Brütsch (p. 27) disagrees with the position of R. Gutzwiller (*Herr der Herrscher, Christus in der geheimen Offenbarung*, Einsiedeln, 1941, p. 60). The time would be described as close for each individual, because each person's life is short. He even goes so far as to suppose (ibid.) that the Apocalypse may have been written as a means of re-awakening a fainting hope in the second coming of Christ. On the other hand, with regard to the phrase "Behold, He *comes* with the clouds" of 1: 7, he also notes (p. 29), that the verb is in the present tense (*ERCHETAI*), although the future would be more normal, as it is, e.gr., in the Apostles' Creed. Brütsch accordingly subscribes to the statement of F. Godet (*Études Bibliques*, 2nd series, Nouveau Testament, Paris, 1874, p. 331), that "The coming of Christ has taken place all through the present age."

Brütsch remarks (pp. 245-246) how the Apocalypse differs from the other biblical writings in its attitude toward Rome. First Maccabees, for example, is most cordial toward the Senate and people of Rome. Christ, Himself declares that his countrymen must render to Caesar the things that are Caesar's. In Rom 13, St. Paul exhorts his readers to be submissive to the authorities (i.e., to Nero and his court, who are anything but favorable to Christ and the Gospel). On the contrary, the Apocalypse author boldly predicts the castigation and eventual destruction of Rome. And his ringing announcement is not at all the word of a barbarian or fanatic of unpolished speech; rather it is the product of a conviction that there can be only irreconcilable antagonism between the emperors, who claim the honors due to divinity, and the Church of Jesus Christ.

The commentary of E. F. Scott is a fine, interesting study of the doctrine of the Apocalypse and of its perduring value. John has rightly seen in the cult of the emperors an affront to the royal dignity of the glorified Christ, and a supreme attempt by Satan to make the order of earthly things the highest order. Thus he sees the present troubles as leading to greater calamities, and calls upon his fellow Christians to be prepared even for martyrdom. There is, of course, no comparison between the tiny handful of defenseless Christians on the one hand, and the vast resources of the Roman empire on the other. Still, John proclaims his conviction that the spiritual forces will be victorious; and history has proven that he was correct!

Thus the Apocalypse, written during a time of crisis, is eminently fitting to periods of crisis and trouble. Even nowadays, while the Church stands apparently helpless in the face of totalitarian states equipped with seemingly unlimited material force, John's Apocalypse seems more fitting than ever. We need only be on guard against the temptations to look in it for precise historical predictions which the author has not the least intention or desire of conveying.

In the corresponding section of the *Bible de Jérusalem*, (pp. 22-26), and also in *Introduction á la Bible*, (tome II, pp. 730-738), Fr. Boismard offers an excellent synthesis of the main doctrinal elements of the Apocalypse. Like many others, he holds that the strictly eschatological doctrine of the Apocalypse is quite little, i.e., that God promises to men a new world in which He will wipe every tear from their eyes; before the inauguration of this perfect Kingdom, all the dead will rise and undergo judgment in accordance with their works; preceding this general resurrection and inauguration of the Kingdom will come the offensive by the Church against the united forces of paganism (Gog amd Magog); the final victory of the Church (the "beloved city") will be brought about without fail through a special intervention of God.

SPECIAL STUDIES

In a work published in 1940, and often reprinted, *The Relevance of Apocalyptic, A study of Jewish and Christian Apocalypses from Daniel to the Revelation* (London), H. H. Rowley places St. John's Apocalypse in its context with other Apocalypse literature, and seeks to distill the doctrine which is common to all these works, i.e., that God directs the course of history according to a plan which He intends to see through to its completion, and that parallel to this divine plan there is also the deliberate scheming of the evil one, whom, of course, God will eventually overcome. Rowley also places considerable emphasis on the Book of Daniel, and on the whole Johannine thought pattern, concluding that it is by no means an accident that these are the only two apocalyptic works to be included in the Canon.

H. M. Fáret offers an excellent idea of the Apocalypse's doctrinal riches, in his *L'Apocalypse de saint Jean. Vision chrétienne de l'histoire*, Paris, 1943. There are, however, some points of interpretation over which we would disagree, (e.gr., the question of the millenium, cf. the last chapter of this study, infra). He cites as the basic points of this New Testament masterpiece, the certitude of the mysterious presence of the risen Christ in the Church, (not merely as an abstract dogma, such as the immortality of the soul, but as actively working in the unfolding of human history); the satanic origin of the persecutions directed against the Church; an obligation incumbent upon Christians to be actively engaged in this struggle; the incompatibility of full Christian life with an attitude of quietism or of detached waiting for an imminent Parousia. Fr. Fáret's work is well complemented by that of J. Comblin, *La résurrection de Jésus Christ*, (Paris, 1958), who has also done a monograph, *La Liturgie de la Nouvelle Jérusalem* (XXI:1 - XXII:5), in ETL, 1953, pp. 5-40. Cf. also on this subject *La Nueva Jerusalem del Apoc. 21:1 seq.*, Cult B, 115 (1953), pp. 359-362; *Dans l'Attente de la nouvelle Jerusalem* in *Lumière et Vie* (*Supplement Biblique de Paroisse et Liturgie*, Bruges) 45, 1959, pp. 1-9.

O. Cullmann, in his study *La royauté du Christ et l'Eglise du Nouveau Testament*, in *Cahier de Foi et Vie* (Paris, 1941), believes that there should be a distinction made between the Kingdom of Christ, which will end at the end of time, and that of God, which will succeed it. Cf. also A. Skrinjar, *Apocalypsis, de Regno Christi*, VD, 1954, p. 289-295.

The main point of the work of M. Rissi, in *Zeit und Geschichte in der Offenbarung des Johannes*, Zürich, 1952, is that the Apocalypse is essentially not a work of abstract theology, but rather a theology of history. Rissi demonstrates that John's Apocalypse is specifically Christian, insofar as, unlike the Jewish Apocalypses, which look only to the future, it looks for the second coming of Christ as related to the former coming, and maintains that salvation has already been effected, through Christ's historical activity, birth, redemptive passion, resurrection, and heavenly exaltation. Because of Christ, those who have faith in Him already live the life of the end time, which is the time of Christ, dominated by His victory over the Evil one and of the activity of the Spirit; this time is also the time of the anti-Christ, whose evil power is presently incarnate in the Roman empire; finally this is the time of the Church, represented by the 144,000 faithful of chapters 7 and 14, and by the woman of chapter 12.

We should mention the work of R. Gutzwiller, *Herr der Herrscher, Christus in der geheimen Offenbarung,* (Einsiedeln - Zürich - Köln, 1951), who maintains that the descriptions originally applied to St. John's own era, are valid for the Church of all times. E. Schmitt, *Die christologische Interpretation als das Grundlegende der Apokalypse,* in ThQ, 1960, p. 257-290, holds that Apocalypse interpretation must be basically Christological. Häring, *Die Botschaft der Offenbarung des Heiligen Johannes,* Munich, 1953, rejects the *zeitgeschichtlich theory,* and offers a much broader interpretation, which, he says, should be primarily eschatological. L. Goppelt (*Heilsoffenbarung und Geschichte nach der Offenbarung des Johannes*), Th Lit Z, 1952, pp. 513-522, emphasizes the Apocalypse's ecclesial import, as does also H. Schlier, *Zum Verständnis der Geschichte nach der Offenbarung Johannis,* in *Die Zeit der Kirche, Exegetische Aufsätze und Vorträge,* Fribourg, 1959, pp. 265-274.

In our study, *Le temps de l'Eglise d'après le Quatrième Evangile et l'Apocalypse* (*La Maison - Dieu,* no. 651, 1961, p. 60-79) we show that the Apocalypse is a necessary complement to St. John's Gospel. Just as the Gospel is oriented entirely toward Jesus' hour, which is also the hour of the Church and of the Sacraments, so also John's Apocalypse shows that this time of the Church is also the time of the presence of the risen Christ in human history. Thus the destiny of man rests, not in the hands of totalitarian despots, but in those of Christ, who alone holds the sealed book, and who alone is able to open it.

In *Gemeinde und Gemeinde-Ordnung im Neuen Testament*, Zürich, 1959, p. 117-122, E. Schweitzer shows that the Church is conceived in the Apocalypse as a supra-historical reality, living now in the desert, but also directly under the influence of its risen Master, Who is constantly present to it. Thus the same antithesis is present here as in the other Johannine texts.

There is a good synthesis of this important question in the article of H. Crouzel, *Le dogme de la Rédemption dans l'Apocalypse*, in Bull L E, 1957, p. 66-92. Also at the end of a work entitled *Mystère des Juifs et des Gentils dans l'Église*, (Paris, no date), E. Peterson speaks of the spirit of the Apostolic Church according to the Apocalypse (pp. 73-102). On the beatitudes of the Apocalypse, cf. W. Bieder, *Die sieben Seligpreisungen in der Offenbarung des Johannes*, in ThZ, 1954, p. 13-30.

In *Lumiere et Vie*, no. 5, 1952, pp. 111-118, Fr. Boismard's article, *Tu enfanteras dans la souffrance; Introduction á la lecture de l'Apocalypse*, shows the leitmotiv of the second prophetic part of the Apocalypse, and also the sources which the author used. In *Mélanges A. Wikenhauser, Synoptische Studien*, (Munich, 1953, pp. 53-63), Fr. Boismard offers another article *Rapprochements literaires entre l'Evangile de Luc et l'Apocalypse*, in which he compares, from the point of view of ideas and of terminology, Luke 4: 1-13 with Apoc. 13; Luke 10: 17-20 with Apoc. 9: 1; 12: 9; 20: 1-3; Luke 22: 31 with Apoc. 2: 10.

Several exegetes have done studies of the attitude of the Apocalypse author toward the civil authorities. Cf. e. gr., L. Brun, *Die römischen Kaiser in der Apok.*, ZNW, 1927, pp. 128-151; E. Stauffer, *Christus und die Caesaren*, Hamburg, 1952, pp. 160-209; O. Cullmann, *Dieu et César*, Neuchâtel - Paris, 1956, pp. 77-90; L. Cerfaux, *Le conflit entre*

Dieu et le souverain divinisé dans L'Apocalypse de Jean, in
*Regalitá Sacra; Contributo al tema dell' VIII Congresso
Internazionale di Storia delle Religioni* (Rome, April, 1955);
H. Schlier, *Vom Antichrist; Zum* 13. *Kapitel der Offenbarung
Johannis,* in *Die Zeit der Kirche,* Freiburg, 1958, pp. 16-29.

A. T. Hanson offers a fine work, *The Wrath of the Lamb,*
(London, 1957), in which he opposes the idea (pp. 159-180)
that the Parousia is never envisioned apart from a manifesta-
tion of God's anger, which, he says, has been present throughout all history, and which John has Christianized by uniting
it to the Cross. Thus Christ's victory has been won only with
the price of the shedding of His blood, and Christians likewise can be victorious by undergoing martyrdom. Even the
frightening descriptions of the judgment in 14: 14-20 and
19: 11-16, recall Calvary, and describe the historical consequences flowing from the rejection of the Messiah.

There is frequent reference, and always positive, to martyrdom, in the Apocalypse (2: 20; 13: 11-15; 17: 6; 18: 4;
19: 1; 20: 4), although the word *MARTYS* in these passages
does not necessarily refer to those who render their testimony
or witness to Christ by shedding their blood. On this point
Cf. E. Günther, *Zeuge und Martyrer,* ZNW, 1956, pp. 145-
161.

The following articles treat only some scattered generalities: G. M. Perella, *Il trionfo della Chiesa nell'Apocalisse,*
in *Divus Thomas,* 43, 1940, p. 324-338; M. Meinertz, *Wesen
und Bedeutung der Johannesapokalypse, Bibel und Kirche*
(Stuttgart), I (1955), pp. 3-13; W. Koester, *Lamm und
Kirche in der Apokalypse,* in *Wort des Lebens (Festschrift
für Meinertz),* 1951, pp. 152-164; I. Fransen, *Jésus le Témoin
Fidéle,* in BVChr, 16, 1956, pp. 66-79; G. Priero, *La Grazia
nell' Apocalisse* in Pal Cl, 35, 1956, p. 703-706; 887-890;
937-952; A. Romeo, *Anticristo,* in *Enciclopedia Cattolica*

Italiana, vol. I, col. 1433-1441; J. Ponthot, (*"Le Seigneur reviendra"*), *Actualité de l'Apocalypse*, in *Revue Diocésaine de Tournai*, 12, 1957, p. 337-342.

The following monographs treat of the few allusions given in the Apocalypse, to the priesthood of Christ and of the faithful: C. Spicq, *L'origine johannique de la conception du Christ Prêtre dans l'Epitre aux Hebreux*, in *Aux sources de la Tradition Chrétienne; Mélanges offerts á M. Goguel*, Neuchâtel - Paris, 1950, pp. 258-269; L. Pelland, *Le sacerdoce des fidèles*, in ScE, 2, 1949, p. 5-26; W. H. Brownlee, *The Priestly Character of the Church in the Apocalypse*, NTS, 5, (1959), p. 224-225.

John's Apocalypse has quite a bit about angels. J. Michl, in his doctoral thesis, *Die Engel um Gott* (München, 1937), treats of some of the more difficult aspects of this Johannine angelology. The four living creatures of Apocalypse 4: 6-8 are an entirely original amalgamation of Isaia's *Seraphim*, and of Ezechiel's *Cherubim*. These creatures have as their principal function to offer praise to God; there is no connection between these angels and any of the elements of astrology or of mythology. The seven spirits of 1: 4 are not a symbol of the seven gifts of the Holy Spirit; rather they are the seven angels which, according to Jewish tradition, are always before Jahweh's face. They appear again in 3: 1; 4: 5, and 5: 6, and in the trumpet blasts of chapters 8-11, and are distinct from the lesser beings who empty out the seven bowls. Of course, these conclusions of Michl are not acceptable to all, but they indicate that he has studied a vast quantity of literature, and for this reason, as well as for many other ones, his work is worthy of serious attention. This work would conceivably be a prototype of others yet to be done on such problematic elements of the Apocalypse as its angelology.

Michl sees angels in the figure of the four living creatures of 4: 5-8 and the seven spirits of 1: 4; however, he insists that such is not the case with regard to the 24 elders of 4: 4, 10; 5: 6, 7, 11, 14; 7: 11, 13; 11: 16; 14: 3; 19: 4. He develops this point in his fine work, *Die 24 Altesten in der Apokalypse des hl Johannes,* (München, 1938). He admits that white robes could pertain to angels as well as to men; however, he insists that nowhere in Scripture do we find men crowned and seated upon thrones. The elders of the Apocalypse must be glorified men; their white robes and golden crowns symbolize victory. Furthermore, since they are clearly distinct from the martyrs and from the multitude of the redeemed, they must be none other than saints of the Old Testament.

P. Benoit considers Michl's position "quite likely," in his very complimentary review of it in RB 1940, pp. 282-284. Wikenhauser follows it in his commentary. Earlier, Skrinjar had arrived at partly the same conclusion, in *Vigintiquattuor Seniores,* in VD 1936, pp. 333-338 and 361-368. We too have taken a similar position in *Les vingt-quatre vieillards de l'Apocalypse,* RB 1958 pp. 5-32, and reproduced in *Études Johanniques,* Bruges - Paris, 1962, pp. 193-227 (English edition *Johannine Studies,* New York, 1964). Bornkamm, on the other hand, in Kittel's TWNT, tome VI, articles on *PRESBYS,* pp. 668-670, refutes Michl's position, maintaining that in the Old Testament and in the apocalyptic literature in general, there is often a figure of an angelic court, acting in a sort of deliberative capacity in heaven.

More and more attention is being given in recent studies to the obviously pronounced liturgical character of the Apocalypse. Some interesting observations are in E. Peterson's *HEIS THEOS, Epigraphische, formgeschichtliche und religionsgeschichtliche Untersuchungen,* Göttingen, 1926: M. Albertz, *Botschaft des Neuen Testaments*, I. Band II. Halbband, *Die Entstehung des Apostolischen Schriftenkanons*, Zürich, 1952, p. 346 sq. 363 ff. Cf. also on this point J. Peschek, *Geheime Offenbarung und Tempeldienst*, Paderborn, 1929; who maintains that the structure of the Apocalypse seems to correspond to the unfolding of a liturgical ceremony in the Jerusalem Temple: opening with the Temple (3: 7); entry into which holy place and daily offering of the lamb (4-5); reading of the Scripture, followed by a commentary (6-7); silent prayer following the readings (8: 1), etc. See also B. Brinkmann, *De visione liturgica in Apocalypsi Sancti Johannis*, VD, 1931, p. 331-342; O. A. Piper, *The Apocalypse of John and the Liturgy of the Ancient Church* in *Church History*, 20 (1951), p. 10-22; L. Mowry, *Revelation IV-V and Early Christian Liturgical Usage*, JBL, 1952, pp. 75-84; A. Cabaniss, *A Note on the Liturgy of Apocalypse*, Interpretation, 1952, p. 78-86; T. F. Torrance, *Liturgie et Apocalypse*, in Verbum Caro II (1957), p. 28-40; A. Feuillet, *Les vingt-quatre vieillards de l'Apocalypse*, RB, 1958 p. 5-32; G. Delling, *Zum Gottesdienstlichen Stil der Johannes Apokalypse*, in NT, 3 (1959), p. 107-137; S. Lauchli, *Eine Gottesdienststruktur in der Johannesoffenbarung*, in Th Z, 16 (1960), p. 359-378. According to M. H. Shepherd, *The Paschal Liturgy and the Apocalypse*, (London, 1960), the structure of the Apocalypse is closely related to the development of the Paschal liturgy, as it was in the churches of Asia; the preparation of the catechumens (the *scrutinia*) thus would correspond to the septet of the letters; the Paschal vigil would correspond to chapters 4 and 5, which depict the assembly before the throne of God; the seals of chapter 6 would correspond to the readings; the signing of the martyrs clothed in white, (chapter 7), would parallel the initiation; chapters 8-18, would correspond to the various parts of the *SYNAXIS*, while, finally, chapters 19-21 (the wedding feast of the Lamb) would be the counterpart to chapter 1. The reserved attitude which the ancient Greek Church maintained in the face of the Apocalypse, did not, however, hinder it (the Apocalypse) from exercising considerable influence upon its liturgy. This is shown by P. Bratsiotis, *L'Apocalypse de saint Jean dans le culte de l'Eglise grecque orthodoxe*, RHPR, 42, (1962), pp. 116-121.

As for the relationship of a doctrinal nature between the Apocalypse and the Epistle to the Hebrews, C. Spicq offers abundant material, and also a very generous documentation, in *L'Epitre aux Hebreux*, Tome I, Introduction (Paris, 1958), pp. 109-138. On the relationship between the Apocalypse and the Song of Songs, especially between Apoc. 3: 20 and Cant. 5: 2; Apoc. 12: 1 and Cant. 6: 10, cf. A. Feuillet, *Le Cantique des Cantiques et l'Apocalypse*, RSR, 1961, p. 321-353.

CONCLUSION

1. *The Christian Meaning of History*

The Apocalypse holds a particular interest for us because of its constant use of Old Testament oracles, re-reading them in the light of the new meaning which they acquire because of Christ, and also because of the message of consolation and encouragement which it strives earnestly to present; i.e., that the Church is sure to win because Christ, its Head, is absolute King of the world who has been victorious over even hostile forces.

To the prophets of Israel is due the eternal glory of having been first to preach, along with strict monotheism, a religious view of history which might well be described as without peer in the entire ancient world. (cf. Procksch,

Iesaja, I, Leipzig, 1930, p. 13). Isaia, especially, opposes the schemes of politicians and of conquerors, by defending the plan of Jahweh, which can be ignored but not thwarted. According to this prince of the prophets, Jahweh is intimately associated with everything that occurs in the life of man. Always immanent to the history of the world, which at the same time He infinitely transcends, in it and by it, He goes on doing His "work." The Apocalypse is thus presented as the Christian fulfillment of ancient prophecy. Like Isaia, Jeremia and Ezechiel before him, John is also called upon to prophesy in a concrete set of circumstances. In John's case, however, the call comes not from Jahweh, as in the lives of the Old Testament prophets; rather, John's call is from the glorious risen Christ; the call comes to him on the "day of the Lord" (1: 9, the first mention of Sunday, day of Christ's Resurrection).

Some authors have wrongly held John's Apocalypse to be more Jewish than Christian, breathing a spirit of revenge rather than the peaceful air of the Sermon of the Mount. In actual fact, the Apocalypse is a thoroughly and authentically Christian work, but a *unilateral* one, written for a period of crisis, and addressed to a Christian community being subjected to a terrible ordeal, for the purpose of bolstering its threatened spirit. As E. F. Scott holds (*The Book of Revelation* pp. 131-132), the first duty of citizens is to defend the fatherland; treason is thus an unpardonable crime. Likewise, St. John reduces all the duties of the Christian to that of absolute fidelity to the cause of Christ and of His Church.

The Apocalypse does not at all seek to soothe its readers by dulling illusions of peace; rather, the author shows the life of the Church as endlessly plagued by terrible crimes of every kind, bringing thereby a needed counterbalance to the naive and unjustified self-deception that progress is automatic and imminent for the Church. The author announces, rather, that the diabolical Beast may kill Christians, while teaching at the same time that it is by being immolated, not by bearing arms (cf. 13: 9-10), that the martyrs followed Christ's example, and won the victory over Satan and his hordes. Charles and Loisy exaggerate when they state that the Apocalypse is nothing but a lengthy invitation to Christians to submit themselves to the test of martyrdom, which, according to 13: 15, is to be meted out to those who refuse to adore the Beast. Allo says well:

> St. John certainly was anxious to lift the members of the seven churches to a high pitch of fervor and fidelity, so that they will be happy to render the witness of death for the cause of Christ; however, he did not think that all *must* be placed in a position to expect it.

Ordinarily, the philosopher of history studies the present in terms of the past, seeking to find in bygone events (wars, revolutions, catastrophes, etc.) some general norms or universally valid laws which he can apply to his own period. The biblical prophets, however, as also the apocalyptic writers, and the author of our inspired New Testament Apocalypse, seek to explain the present in terms of the future, looking forward to the eventual final fulfillment which alone can explain the sense of present events. The Church had grown well since its foundation, but now, in the days in which John writes his work, the forces of evil are threatening the Church with nothing short of extinction. John shows how the Church's present trials, the face of a totalitarian state possessed of irresistible material strength, all fit into God's plan; He even goes so far as to foretell what will be the eventual outcome of this divine plan. Because the master of history is not the Emperor of Rome, but the risen Christ, these frightful attacks against the Church are only the last desperate assaults of the dragon, who is already vanquished, and mortally wounded.

Thus the Apocalypse brings to Christians of every age *the basic meaning of the Church's History;* i.e., that it is the presence in history of the risen Christ, who works through the Holy Spirit (in the letters of chapters 2 and 3, there is really only one message, presented as that of both Christ and the Spirit). It is also the time in which the power of Satan, already mortally wounded, fights on desperately, using human aid (symbols of the two beasts of chapter 13); there will also be periods of calm (cf. below on the reign of 1000 years), before the final attack on the Church which God will eventually frustrate.

2. *Christian Re-reading of the Old Testament*

These doctrines are, of course, of the most fundamental importance. As a matter of fact, many exegetes have gone so far as to maintain that without the Apocalypse the New Testament would be incomplete. Whereas the other texts of the New Testament deal with the Christian community taken in itself, the Apocalypse shows the Church in its relationship with pagan nations around about it, and describes its existence in terms of the entire history of the world. In this regard the Apocalypse ranks among the works of the great prophets, especially first and second Isaia, and is justly called the Book of Daniel of Christianity.

St. John's Apocalypse could well be defined as a rereading of the Old Testament in the light of the events of

Christian history. In this sense it is, true enough, not the most interesting or attractive of the New Testament books. The author never makes a single quotation, which is unusual in this sort of literary style. Nevertheless, most of the verses (278 out of 404, according to Westcott-Hort) do contain at least one, and often several, allusions to Scripture, especially to the prophetic texts (particularly to Isaia, Jeremia, Ezechiel, Daniel, and Zacharia), as well as to the Psalms, to Genesis, and to Exodus. In order to appreciate these references fully, the reader would do well to avail himself of the fine lists of Scriptural citations with which Swete (pp. CXL-CLIII) and Charles (vol. 1, pp. LXV-LXXXVI) have prepared their commentaries. This tendency to explain the Scriptures in the light of present events is also characteristic of the DSS of the Qumran Community (the Peshers of Habacuc, and Nahum, and prayers of Thanksgiving). In the early conflicts between Christianity and Judaism the manner of referring to the Old Testament showed that Christ's life and death were in conformity with the ancient pronouncements. In the Apocalypse this method serves to show that the Church's history unfolds in conformity with the teachings of the Sacred Scriptures, as did the life of its divine Founder.

Going even more deeply into the mind of the Apocalypse author, we see that this Christian re-reading of the Old Testament derives from the profound conviction that the real meaning of the Old Testament becomes evident only in and through Christ. As C. H. Dodd has emphasized in his book *History and the Gospel*, (London, 1952, pp. 32 ff), one of the basic characteristics of the Old Testament is that God's plan is never seen therein as accomplished or brought to fulfillment in the history of Israel. The New Testament writers, on the other hand, and the Apocalypse author in

particular, show their conviction that, thanks to the coming
of Christ to earth, the ancient prophecies have been realized.
Consequently, there is no longer to be any waiting; the
climax, the summit, toward which all history has been
oriented by God, the *OMEGA* which explains the *ALPHA*,
has come and has its place in Jesus. Thus it is no accident
that the Apocalypse alludes so strongly to the first chapters
of the Bible. Not only the oracles of the prophets, but also
the opening pages of Genesis become fully intelligible only
when they are read in the light of the redemptive Incarnation.

It seems now that this deliberate use of the Old Testament, which the Apocalypse author makes, should be studied
more carefully than has been the case so far. There are two
points in particular which need clarification; first, are these
Old Testament citations taken from the Hebrew, or from
the Greek, or perhaps from some Greek version other than
the Septuagint (cf. A. Vanhoye, *L'utilisation du livre d'Ezé-
chiel dans l'Apocalypse*, Bib. 1962, pp. 436-476)? Secondly,
can we say that the author, leaning as heavily as he does
upon the earlier writings, manages nevertheless to maintain
his own originality? We think that he does. As a matter of
fact, the more one studies the Apocalypse, the more one
comes to admire the masterful control with which the sacred
author uses his sources, adopting and adapting them, fitting
them into the scheme. He needs to effect only the slightest
modifications, in order to bring out, by symbols or Old
Testament phrases, his own distinctively Christian ideas. We
have, then, not a mere mosaic of citations, or a list of disparate texts chosen and arranged at random, but rather a
magnificent literary creation "animated by a single breath"
(according to A. Vanhoye). The frequency of the scriptural
citations is no more opposed to the personal inspiration of
the Apocalypse author than are the literary symbols and

figures which he creates to serve his purpose. Thus the many parts, interconnected and mutually dependent, all come together to form one revelation, one apocalypse, from beginning to end of the Christian fulfillment of the Old Testament. For a more developed presentation of this point of view, cf. E. Hühn, *Die alttestamentlichen Citate und Reminiscenzen im N. T.*, Tübingen, 1900; W. Dittmar, *Vetus Testamentum in Novo*, Göttingen, 1903; cf. also P. Lestringant, *Essai sur l'unité de la révélation biblique*, Paris, 1942, p. 148-154.

3. *The Problem of the Delay of the Parousia*

Still we think that the Apocalypse has a still greater importance because of the fact that it helps to solve in a most original way the formidable problem which weighs upon the thought of Christians, i.e., the delay of the final coming of the Parousia. We have offered some explanations of this question in *Sacra Pagina, Miscellanea Biblica Congressus Internationalis Catholici de Re Biblica* (edited by J. Coppens, A. Descamps, E. Massaux), *volumen alterum*, Paris - Gembloux, 1959, p. 914-929; *Le Chapitre X de l'Apocalypse, son apport dans la solution du problème eschatologique*. Cf. also our article *Parousie* in SDB (cols. 1397-1403).

The tenth chapter of the Apocalypse declares that the end is near; the coming of the Lion of Juda (5: 5) into the midst of the chosen people, and all the judgments which have followed upon it, especially the castigation meted out to the unbelieving Jews (who are represented, we think, by the two septets of seals and the trumpets), have brought mankind close to the end of its own evolution, so that there remains little to look forward to, except the blast of the seventh trumpet. This blast is proclaimed in v. 5-7 with great solemnity (cf. the phrase *CHRONOS OUKETI ESTAI*). The Apocalypse author certainly has no intention of helping to perpetuate this notion of the nearness of the end. Quite the contrary; this idea was for the persecuted Christians, in effect, a source of the greatest consolation.

On the other hand, however, there is here a most intriguing paradox, insofar as chapter 10 of the Apocalypse makes it also abundantly clear that the end of history is still a thing to be awaited only in the distant future. This is the meaning not only of the command addressed to John, to seal up the things that the seven thunders spoke (10: 4), because the fulfillment of them is still a long ways off (cf. also Dan. 8: 26; 12: 4; Apoc. 22: 10), but also of the scene of the Book that has been eaten (vv. 8-11); as Fr. Boismard has pointed out (RB, 1949, pp. 510-511), this scene implies of necessity a whole new series of decrees, which the prophet is to transmit, and which are to be put into effect before the coming of the end. For that matter, all the events of chapters 12-20 (introduced by chapter 10), i.e., the persecution brought on by the Dragon and set in motion by the Beast come out of the sea, the plagues of the bowls, the punishment of Babylon, the victory of the Word of God over the Beast, the reign of Christ and of His witnesses throughout the symbolic thousand years, the final attack of Gog and Magog against the Church,—all this must come to pass before the blast of the last trumpet.

This paradoxical view of an end which is, at one time, near and still in the distant future, which the Apocalypse author presents as none before him have done, draws attention away from the really lesser question of dates, even though this element has been predominant in exegesis. The original Christian readers of the passage could recall to mind the moment in which Christ foretold both the terrify-

ing destruction of Jerusalem and of the Temple, and the
consoling event of the messianic triumph of the Son of Man,
thereby predicting (as it would seem), the end of the world
in the strict sense, and His own Parousia. Doubtless it was
the catastrophe of 70 which had provoked the denial of the
Parousia, and against which the second Epistle of St. Peter
was written (cf. J. Chaine, *Les Épitres Catholiques*, Paris,
1939, pp. 33-34). Thus the author of the Apocalypse, en-
lightened at once by the Holy Spirit and by the actual
life lived by the Church, understood even better than the
other New Testament writers, the danger to be avoided
with regard to this confusion. For it was clear that the sooner
or later coming of the end is a theological datum, and not
a chronological indication. This point, we are sure, is one
of the most important and precious of the entire New Testament revelation.

4. Christology of the Apocalypse and its Doctrinal Relation to the Rest of the New Testament

Bousset said that the Christology of the Apocalypse is
probably the richest of the entire New Testament. There is,
accordingly, good reason why we should apply more effort
than has been done heretofore, to the study of the imagery
and the formulas by which it is expressed. One might say
that this Christology recalls at once all the teachings of
St. Paul, especially in the Captivity Epistles, and also the
teachings of the fourth Gospel. Jesus is the first-born of the
dead (1: 5): the First and the Last (1: 18); He who lives
(1: 18); the holy one, the true one (3: 7); the beginning
of the creation of God (3: 14); the word of God (19: 13);
He is King and Priest (cf. the introductory vision of 1: 12 ff).

Paradoxically enough, he is at one time both the Lion of the tribe of Juda (5: 5) and the Lamb who was slain (there are 29 occurrences of the Lamb who was slain, in the Apocalypse), who appears to the Seer "as if slain" (5: 6) bearing the marks of his sacrifice (the victory over death comes to him only because of Calvary). We might quote here the words of Victorinus, *ad devincendum mortem leo, ad patiendum vero pro hominibus tamquam agnus ad occisionem ductus est.* Similarly the author of the fourth Gospel (20: 20, 21, 25, 27; cf. also Luke 24: 20), emphasizes that the risen Christ retains the scars of His wounds forever. The meaning of these wounds is the same in the Apocalypse and the Gospel, i.e., the scars are a sign of the permanence of Christ's redemptive love. In other words, faithful Christians have nothing to fear; every moment in the Church, the redemptive love which brought about Calvary, is available to them, to give them life. In Apocalypse 22: 1, the river of the water of life "clear as crystal" which comes forth from the throne of God and of the Lamb, is obviously related to the rivers of the living water of John 7: 38-39, and the blood and water which flow forth from the pierced side of the crucified Savior in John 19: 33-37.

We could profit also from consideration of the undeniable theological affinities existing between the Apocalypse and the Epistle to the Hebrews. In either case we have an earnest exhortation to be constant in the face of trials; in either case, suffering Christians are admonished to look upward to heaven; furthermore, each of the two documents speaks of a heavenly liturgy. The powerful picture of the heavenly Jerusalem in Heb. 12: 18-24, is quite like that which presents itself to the gaze of the Seer of Apocalypse 21. In Heb. 11: 2, the saints of the Old Testament dispensation are called "men of old" (*PRESBYTEROI*), clearly distinct from the Christians of the present time, and intensely interested in the conflicts which face the disciples on earth (cf. 12: 1). We are of the opinion that these elements are a useful key to the identification of the 24 elders or ancients, who are mentioned no less than a dozen times in the Johannine writings.

In spite of these many points of similarity, it seems unwarranted to conclude to a direct influence of Heb. on the Apocalypse. The Apocalypse author, who could have had at his disposal several writings of the apostolic corpus (according to Charles, vol. 1, p. LXXXIII, ff., Mt.; Lk.; 1 Th.; 1 and 2 Cor.; Col.; Ephes., and possibly Gal.; 1 Peter and James), nevertheless does not seem to have relied on Hebrews to any definite extent.

It would be most interesting, we think, to study in detail the relationships of vocabulary and thought patterns, existing between the Apocalypse and the Pastoral Epistles. A formula as emphatic as that of 1 Tim. 6: 15, "King of kings and Lord of Lords," recalls similar expressions applied to Jahweh in the Old Testament, but has New Testament parallels only in the Apocalypse, in which we can clearly detect an attitude of hostility toward the Emperor, "ruler of the kings of the earth" (1: 5); "Lord of lords and King of kings" (17: 14); "King of kings and Lord of lords" (19: 16). For both the Apocalypse author and the writer of the Pastorals, only Christ is "the great God and Savior" of Christians (Titus 2: 13). Furthermore, the theological vocabulary of the Pastorals has a manifestly Johannine color, as is evident from the use of such words as *MARTYREIN; PHŌTIZEIN; PHAN-EROUN; DEIKNYNAI; KOSMOS; TĒREIN; ENTOLĒ.*

5. Liturgical Character of the Apocalypse

We should be on guard against the danger of misunderstanding with regard to the Apocalypse's liturgical character. True enough, it is not a specifically or professedly liturgical document, but rather a prophecy and an account of visions. Still, we must not lose sight of its liturgical aspects, which have been emphasized, and placed very much in relief, although not always discreetly, by modern exegetes. As is the case of the Gospel, (cf. especially chapters 17 and 19), the Christ of the Apocalypse is King and Priest together (cf. 1: 12-16), and he makes his faithful witnesses to be kings and priests also (1: 6; 5: 20; 20: 6). Most of the great visions of the Apocalypse have some sort of liturgical flavor to them, which is due basically to the essentially eschatological orientation characteristic of the Christian liturgy, especially of the eucharist, in which we "announce the death of the Lord until He comes" (1 Cor. 11: 26; cf. also Didache, chapters 9 and 10). As a memorial of the Passion and Resurrection of Christ, the eucharistic celebration guarantees the actual presence of Christ in His Church, as a sign of the definitive union of the Lover and the Beloved, in the celebration of the eternal union of heaven (cf. O. Cullmann, *Le Culte dans L'Église Primitive*, Neuchâtel - Paris, 1945, pp. 12-15, and the reference to the eucharist in the ancient prayer, *Maranatha*, reproduced at the end of the Apocalypse, 22: 20).

It follows from this that John, wishing to express the Church's profound eschatological hope, describes it under the form of a heavenly liturgy, availing himself of some formulas and images which he has borrowed from the liturgies of the old and new Covenants. This explains the use of the various doxologies, acclamations, and hymns, which appear scattered throughout the Johannine texts, without any precise indications as to whether they are direct borrowings, or perhaps deliberate imitations, at least in some cases (cf. 1: 5-8; 4: 8-11; 5: 8-9, 12-13; 11: 15; 12: 10-12; 14: 7; 15: 3-4; 16: 5; 19: 7; 22: 17). The chant is, of course, an expression of joy, and is particularly fitting for thanksgiving, and is a basic element of the Church's traditional usage. Here it is used especially to praise Christ as Redeemer, both in heaven and on earth. The celebration of this magnificent liturgy is set within the framework of a heavenly Temple, which is obviously the antitype of the Jerusalem Temple, and which opens up after the disappearance of the Jewish earthly sanctuary, to reveal the presence of the ark of the new Covenant (11: 19). In this Temple there is an altar, which recalls the altar of burnt offerings (6: 9; 8: 3; 14: 18; 16: 7) and another altar which recalls the altar of incense. The exclusion of sinners and of pagans from the new Jerusalem in 22: 15 has been likened to the exclusion of infidels and the unworthy from the Christian assembly immediately preparatory to the celebration of the eucharistic mystery. We might note in 1: 6-7 the presence of "amen" and "even so," which indicate the double heritage, Jewish and Greek, reflected in this liturgy. The "alleluia" of 19: 1, 3, 4, 6, is also a borrowing from the Jewish liturgy, and is found nowhere else in the New Testament.

We might also mention in this regard a very interesting observation, such as could be forthcoming from future studies on the background and structural plan of the Apocalypse. The letters of St. Ignatius of Antioch show that in the churches of Asia Minor, at the end of the first century, i.e., the time of the composition of the Apocalypse, the churches were governed by bishops with the assistance of a council of elders, or presbyters. "Certain it is that your presbytery, which is a credit to its name, is a credit to God, for it harmonizes with the bishop as completely as the strings of a harp (Eph. 4: 1). The bishop and the presbyters represent together the entire Church (Magn. 2: 1). The *presbyters* owe obedience to their bishop as to the Father of Jesus Christ, who is the bishop of all (Magn. 3: 1). Cf. also Magn. 6: 1; 7: 1; 13: 1; Eph. 4: 1; Trall. 2: 2; 7: 12; 12: 2; 13: 2; Phil. 4: 1, and many other passages of Ignatius.

The Christian readers of the Apocalypse, in coming upon the word *PRESBYTEROI*, would not be at all inclined to think of angels, because in the Scriptures angels are never referred to by that title (not even in Is. 24: 23, according to our opinion). On the contrary, however, it would be entirely natural for them to imagine a sort of privileged elite of the saved in heaven, very much like the picture of the presbyters grouped around about the bishop, whom Ignatius compares precisely to "the Father of Jesus Christ, who is bishop of all." Thus the 24 elders suggest a sort of heavenly presbyterium, grouped around about with God, as it were, in council. The Apocalypse author is trying thus, to show in heaven a sort of prototype of the earthly hierarchy. Lohmeyer observes that in 4: 11 the song of the elders, with the characteristic words, "Worthy art thou," recalls the formula used later on in the ceremony of enthronement of bishops. The historian Socrates, (*Hist. Eccl.* 4: 30), writes that this phrase of acclamation was applied to Ambrose, when he was elected bishop of Milan.

The Apocalypse has been called, although not without some exaggeration, an eschatological liturgy; still it does serve to show us what the real earthly liturgy is, or should be made to be. It has at its base the liturgical forms of the Old Testament, transformed and transfigured by Christ's Passion and Resurrection. Furthermore, it is no more than an anticipated echo, however fragmentary and imperfect, of the great heavenly liturgy of an entirely new creation, of the new heaven and the new earth" (T. F. Torrance).

CHAPTER V

DATE AND PLACE OF COMPOSITION
OF THE APOCALYPSE

THE PROBLEM

Formerly various hypotheses were offered as to the date of the composition of the Apocalypse, ranging from the time of Claudius (41-54) to the reign of Domitian (81-96). Nowadays most commentators accept the word of Irenaeus (*Adv. Haer.* V, 30: 3), that the Apocalypse was written "toward the end of the reign of Domitian," i.e., about 90-96. As for the place, it seems clear from the text itself, that it was the island of Patmos (cf. 1: 9-10), and most exegetes accept this indication. However, it is also noteworthy that, even if we accept the tradition of a protracted stay on Patmos by reason of exile, this does not necessarily mean that the author was there when he began to write of his visions.

We might note also that, strictly speaking, the words with which the Apocalypse describes the stay of John on Patmos, "because of the word of God and the testimony of Jesus," could of themselves refer to no more than a missionary or preaching visit. The more common view, however, is that John was exiled there, especially in view of the phrase of 1: 9, "I, John, your brother and partner in the tribulation." This need not have been necessarily any type of forced labor, nevertheless, given the fact that there were no mines or stone-workers operated there by the imperial government (cf. G. Camps, art. *Patmos,* in SDB, cols. 73-81).

The chief objection which could be raised against the date indicated by Irenaeus, is the Apocalypse passage (17: 9-11), which refers to the 7 heads of the one Beast, "The seven heads are seven mountains, upon which one woman sits (i.e., the 7 hills of Rome); and these are 7 kings; five of them have fallen: one of them is, and the other has not yet come; and when he comes, he must remain a short time. And the beast that was, and is not, is moreover himself eighth, and is of the 7 and is on his way to destruction."

It seems obvious enough, and most commentators agree, that the reference is to 7 kings or emperors, of Rome. The Greek word *BASILEUS* can, of course, refer to the Caesars of Rome (Cf. John 19: 15; I Pet. 2: 13, 17). However, in this case the sixth king (the one reigning at the time in which the author writes *HO HEIS ESTIN*) should be Domitian, if we are to be in harmony with the date offered by Irenaeus. The difficulty is that, if we count the Emperors, beginning with Augustus, the sixth is not Domitian, but Otho or Vespasian, depending on whether or not we accept the brief interregna of Galba, Otho and Vitellius.

We might consider briefly some of the chief explanations which have been proposed to solve this problem. According to Loisy, the author does the same as does Matthew in presenting his genealogy, i.e., he deliberately omits some names, in order to arrive at the number 7 (cf. commentary, ad loc., p. 310). Bonsirven follows Allo partially, in reckoning the Emperors from the time in which the empire, by its declared hostility, has become a wild beast toward the Church, i.e., beginning with the reign of Nero. Baldensperger speaks of successive redactions. Likewise Père Boismard holds a redaction of the Apocalypse in several stages. Thus the second text would be written under Nero, and the first under Vespasian, or at the time of Domitian, and the letters to the seven churches a little later, under Domitian. The Apocalypse would have received its final form about 95, at the beginning of the persecution of Domitian.

Touilleux and Giet, whose studies we mentioned above, both give an original solution to the complex problem of the date of composition of the Apocalypse.

Giet holds that the core of the Apocalypse is the section of the 4 septets of the seals, the trumpets, the visions (chapters 12-15), and the bowls. These septets are to be dated about 74-75. The 7 heads (7 kings) and 10 horns (10 kings) of the Beast (13: 1; 17: 9-12) are to be explained in the light of Josephus, who counts the Roman Emperors beginning with Caesar inclusively, without counting the three short reigns of Galba, Otho, and Vitellius. The emperor who has not yet come (17: 10) is Nero; the one presently reigning is Vespasian; the 10 kings of 17: 12 are the 7 emperors from Caesar to Vespasian, plus the three emperors of the Interregnum.

We hasten to say that this last explanation seems improbable. The period which corresponds best of all to the composition of he Apocalypse is not the reign of Vespasian, but that of Domitian. This date rests not only on the explicit witness of Irenaeus, but also on the weighty fact that the adoration of the Beast under penalty of death, which is deprecated in chapter 13, is a perfect characterization of the acts of Domitian. On this subject cf. E. Stauffer, *Christus und die Caesaren,* Hamburg, 1952, pp. 160-209 (*Domitian und Johannes*); cf. also the study of L. Cerfaux and J. Tondriau, *Le Culte des Souverains,* Paris - Tournai, 1957, pp. 355-357.

Touilleux's suggestions are of interest because they bring

into consideration all the elements of the problem. The interpretation of 17: 10 is based on the principle that, instead of devising a way of counting the Emperors that would make the list end with Domitian, it would be better to look to see how an Oriental would understand the Passage. The most normal way would be to begin with Augustus, not counting the three reigns of 69, and arriving thereby, not at Domitian as the sixth Emperor, but at Vespasian. In order to bring this last element into harmony with the traditional dating (the reign of Domitian), we need merely refer to a practice common among apocalyptic writers, i.e., that of fictitious ante-dating.

CONCLUSION

As soon as we accept the usual and normal way of counting the Emperors of 17: 10, which is used by most commentators (Holtzmann, Swete, Charles, Gelin, Kiddle, Cerfaux, and Cambier), we find ourselves virtually compelled to accept the hypothesis of fictitious ante-dating. The traditional setting of the Apocalypse in the reign of Domitian is too solidly established to be brought into question.

In our view, the real problem is in determining the influence which this practice of ante-dating should have upon our exegesis of the Apocalypse, and to find the best way of explaining this fictitious practice. Is it true, as Touilleux says it is, that we need to look all through chapters 4 - 11, for references to specific historical events of the years 68-75? We think not. St. John's use of imagery here is quite traditional and conventional, and, after all, the first object of our consideration should be the biblical sources which the author has used.

If one accepts the interpretation offered above for the first prophetic part of the Apocalypse (chapters 4-11), then the practice of fictitious ante-dating, which would otherwise seem strange, becomes quite satisfactory. John's Apocalypse, bearing the author's signature, is not in the fictional style characteristic of the other Jewish apocalypses, which bear the name of an outstanding hero of the distant past. If John uses this means, there is nothing to indicate that he does it in order to deceive his readers, or to lead them to take his oracles as prophecies *ex eventu.* He merely wishes to take a step backward, and to place himself under Vespasian before the destruction of Jerusalem and of the Temple, in order to see the theological significance of this event, the gravest crisis which the Christian community has had to face to date.

The ante-dating would be all the more understandable if we could show that for the last redaction of the Apocalypse John used some fragments written earlier, as many critics have suspected (cf. above). This may possibly be the best explanation of the letters at the beginning of the work. True enough, the septet of the letters has a tone altogether distinct from that of the rest of the book, as Charles and Touilleux have pointed out. There is no mention in this section either of a general persecution (except perhaps in 3: 10), or of emperor-worship. Touilleux explains these omissions by what he calls fundamental fiction. We could also suppose for the letters an original redaction a bit anterior to the date as far as the time of Vespasian (as does Charles).

NOTE

Some authors have tried to determine the date of the Apocalypse from 13: 18, in which John gives the number of the beast (cf., example R. Schütz, *Die Offenbarung des Johannes und Kaiser Domitian,* Göttingen, 1933). In place of the number 666, R. Schütz prefers the variant 616, which is supported by C and Irenaeus (*Adv. Haer.* V. 30, 1.) Schütz is of the opinion that this latter number represents the inscription of Domitian's official seal, in the 16th year of his reign (DCXVI); the first two letters stand for *Domitianus Caesar*, and the three last would refer to the years of the length of his reign. P. Touilleux (op. cit., pp. 88-95), and A. Gelin (*Commentaire*, p. 636), have both been very favorably impressed by this hypothesis. Given the plausibility of this explanation, the problem would be solved.

But Schütz's opinion is far from immune to criticism. (cf. Allo, RB, in 1936, p. 589). In general, to attempt to date the Apocalypse by 13: 18 seems to be explaining the obscure by the more obscure. Most commentators are satisfied to follow the good reading of 666, but, even then, they have devised all sorts of methods to explain this figure, such as a symbolic meaning, a triangular meaning, *isopsephe*, (i.e., juxtaposition of two names which have letters bearing the same numerical value, example, Caesar, Nero, and THĒRION [beast]), etc. Nowadays, the most common explanation is gematry, a practice common in antiquity and well known to the Jews. However, even given the possibility of such a method in John's mind, we do not know whether he would have counted more probably in Greek or in Hebrew letters. All in all, the best thing is probably to admit that we will very likely never know the identity of the person whom John saw.

CHAPTER VI

THE AUTHOR OF THE APOCALYPSE

THE PROBLEM

At first glance it might seem, perhaps, that the problem of authorship is settled by the Apocalypse text itself, insofar as the author who describes his visions, calls himself John (1: 1; 4: 9; 22: 8), and places himself among the prophets (22: 9). But who is this John? Is he the Apostle? or could he be a John other than the beloved Apostle? Is he an anonymous writer who takes the name of one of the sons of Zebedee, in accordance with the apocalyptic practice of the time? In the long run, we shall see that this question of the authorship of the Apocalypse is one of the most trying and most difficult of all biblical problems.

Formerly most commentators held simply that the Apostle John was personally the author of the Apocalypse. Most Catholics still hold this (Allo, Gelin, Vaganay, Braun, Feret, Tillmann, Sickenberger, G. M. Camps); so do several non-Catholic exegetes (Behm, Michaelis, Menoud). In favor of this position they cite the testimony of the most ancient tradition, i.e., that of Justin (*Dialogue with Trypho the Jew* 81: 4), and of Irenaeus (*Adversus Haer.* IV, 21: 11). The opposite opinion arose only later, especially because of the anti-Montanist polemic (Caius, in Eusebius, *Hist. Eccl.*

III, 28: 2), and also because of the need to check the millenarists by disqualifying one of their chief tenets (Denis of
Alexandria, in Eusebius, *Hist. Eccl.* VII: 24).

A new element, which seems to us to be very important,
has only recently come to the fore (cf. A. Helmbold, *A Note
on the Authorship of the Apocalypse,* in NTS, vol. 8., Oct.
1961, pp. 77-79). Since 1896, scholars have been aware of
the existence of the *Apocryphon* (or secret book) of John,
which Irenaeus mentions in *Adversus Haereses.* However, it
was not until 1955 that W. C. Till made available for study
a critical edition of the Berlin manuscript containing the
gnostic text (*die Gnostischen Schriften des koptischen Papyrus Berolinensis* 8502, Berlin, 1955). Also, the gnostic library
discovered in 1945 at Chenoboskion in upper Egypt has
provided us with three different redactions of this same work.
One of these contained in Codex X of the classification of
Doresse, has been reproduced photographically as *Coptic
Gnostic Papyri in the Coptic Museum at Old Cairo,* (Cairo,
1956). Although this latter text differs from the Berlin copy,
still it contains, as does the Berlin text, in the description of
the revelation supposedly reported by John, a whole series
of phrases reminiscent of Apocalypse 1: 13-19, especially
the phrase, "the things that are, and the things that have
been and the things that are to come hereafter," which is
an almost verbatim equivalent of Apocalypse 1: 19. As
happens elsewhere in this kind of literature, in both the
Berlin and in the Chenboskion text, the author presents
himself as the Apostle John, brother of James and son of
Zebedee, which means that he claims to be the same person
as the Seer of the canonical Apocalypse, and that he attributes this latter text to the Apostle John.

The importance of this testimony depends obviously on
the date of the *Apocryphon.* Critics are agreed that it is

ancient, but they differ on the precise date, ranging in general
from the end of the first century to 150; some even go a bit
later. This clearly gives us a very ancient attestation of the
apostolic and Johannine origin of the Apocalypse.

Defenders of the apostolic and Johannine origin of the
Apocalypse appeal also to reasons drawn from the examination of the book itself. Evidently the author is a Christian of
Jewish and Palestinian background. And, since he calls himself John, he could hardly be any other than the Apostle,
since history tells us of no other person of this time (end of
the first century) sufficiently eminent in the Churches of
Asia to speak to them in a tone of such authority.

To this fact they add the many points of grammar, vocabulary, style, and doctrine in the Apocalypse which relate it
to the fourth Gospel. In some densely packed pages, (CXCIX
-CCXXII). Fr. Allo compares the Apocalypse with the
fourth Gospel and with the three Epistles attributed to
John. Along with some undeniable differences, he also
reports some striking resemblances, from the point of view
of language (vocabulary and grammar), of doctrine, of the
mentality which these writings reflect (dramatic character,
love of symbolism and allegory, mystical use of numbers;
polyvalence of symbols, etc.); and finally from the point of
view of the style and manner of composition (constant
parallelism, frequent use of antithesis; insistence on preparations; slow and careful integration of ideas, and musical
progression of themes which "continue to move on and ex-
pand, as it were in waves," and, finally, the ternary rhythm
of developments and elements).

Some exegetes accept only one or other part of the thesis
that the Apostle John is the only author of both the fourth
Gospel, and the Apocalypse. Among the partisans of the
partial thesis (i.e., that the 4th Gospel and the Apocalypse

are from the same author) are E. Lohmeyer, M. Goguel,
(at least to the extent that he once held this view; cf. RHPR,
1931, p. 131). Harnack also held this opinion when re
wrote in 1897, "I share the view of those critics who hold
that the Apocalypse and Gospel are the work of one and the
same author," (*Geschichte der Altchristlichen Literatur bis
Eusebius, II Die Chronologie*, I, 1897, p. 675, no. 1; quoted
by Ph. H. Menoud, *L'Évangile de Jean d'aprés les récher-
ches récentes*, Neuchâtel - Paris, 1947, p, 73).

Other exegetes have held that the Apocalypse could be
the work of the Apostle John but that the Gospel may not
be Johannine. De Wette held this in the past (*Kurze Erklärung der Offenbarung Johannis*, 1862), as did Reuss
(*L'Apocalypse*, 1878), H. J. Holtzmann (*Evangelium, Briefe
und Offenbarung des Johannes*, Freiburg in Breisgau, 1891).
M. Kiddle also holds this opinion.

Now we can consider the arguments offered by the great
number of critics now including some Catholics, (M. E. Boismard, Wikenhauser), who reject, or at least doubt, the
apostolic origin of the Apocalypse, as well as the single
authorship of both the fourth Gospel and of the Apocalypse.

These objections are not entirely new. Denis of Alexandria (in Eusebius, *Hist. Eccl.* VII, 25) offered some. His
line of argument has been resumed and even amplified by
modern critics, e.gr., Loisy, Charles, Baldensperger, Windisch (in RGG, 2nd edition, art. *Johannes Apocalypse*, pp.
330-346), and a number of others considered completely
untenable not only the apostolic origin of the Apocalypse,
but also the attribution of it to the same hand as that of the
author of the 4th Gospel and the Johannine Epistles.

Some of the objections raised are, for example, the fact
that the author never refers to himself as an apostle, whereas
he frequently describes his work as prophetic. Furthermore,

some say, the Apostle John must have been martyred in 44, or else between 62-70; thus he could not have written the Apocalypse. Besides, it is difficult to understand how there could be an almost total absence of any allusions to the Christ of history, if the Apocalypse is the work of the son of Zebedee.

Charles (vol. 1, pp. CXVII-CLX) has written a "short grammar of the Apocalypse," which is most worthy of the attention of the serious reader, containing morphology, (nouns, adjectives, uses of the articles, verb forms, prepositions, etc.); words which can be understood only if translated into Hebrew; Hebraic expressions and constructions, solecisms, etc. All this study leads to the conclusion that, although the language of the Gospel and of the Epistles is correct, the Greek of the Apocalypse "is based on Hebrew, thought in Hebrew, and can be understood and tasted only by those who know Hebrew" (Renan, *L'Antéchrist*, Paris, 1873, p. XXXI). Because of this, many have held, but not proven, that the Apocalypse was first written in Hebrew and later translated into Greek. Cf., e.gr., R. Balgarnie Young Scott, *The Original Language of the Apocalypse*, (Toronto, 1928); M. Mieses, *Hebraische Fragmente aus dem jüdischen Urtext der Apokalypse des hl. Johannes*, in *Monatschrift für Geschichte und Wissenschaft des Judentums*, 74 (1930), pp. 345-362.

From the doctrinal or theological point of view, the Gospel is characterized by the actualization of eternal life and by the considerable use of eschatological perspectives. Aside from this, it does not rely heavily on apocalyptic imagery, such as that of the coming of the Son of Man on the clouds, accompanied by angels amid signs of a terrifying upheaval of the heavens, blowing of trumpets, etc. The Apocalypse itself, on the other hand, is made up, for the most part, of the most colorful and impressive kind of grandiose eschatological tableaux. The most characteristic phrases and key-words of the Gospel and the Epistles, light, darkness, love, truth, the world (in a pejorative sense), are absent or rare in the Apocalypse. Furthermore, even if in both of them Christ is called the *Logos*, still there is a great difference between the cosmic *Logos* of the Gospel and the *Logos* as Avenger, armed with a sword, of the Apocalypse. There is also a great distance between the God of love of the Gospel and of the Epistles, and the terrible God of the Apocalypse, who is the same as the Almighty (*Pantokrator*) of the Old Testament. Only with difficulty do we find in the Apocalypse any allusion to the love which caused God to send His Son into the world. Whereas the Apocalypse is oriented toward the exterior judgment of the end of time, the author of the Gospel sees the judgment as entirely interior, and as being effected in the present. The Apocalypse depicts the world made new at the end of time, by borrowing a set of images from Judaism; the author of the Gospel has a more purely spiritual view, according to which the end of time and its era are simply the "Father's house."

We could, of course, go on and cite many additional instances of basic differences between the Apocalypse and the fourth Gospel and the Johannine Epistles. Renan sums up the situation by saying, "The Apocalypse is the most Jewish, and the fourth Gospel is the least Jewish, of all the writings of the New Testament." (L'Antéchrist, p. XXV).

CONCLUSION

It would be entirely incorrect to consider the question of the authorship of the Apocalypse as closed to all discussion; far from it, it is not at all dogmatically determined, and is open to free study by any member of any faith, not excluding the Catholic. The task remains to be done, of weighing the pros and cons of each line of argument, taking due care to consider all the elements of each question, including the weight of ancient tradition. It would be entirely rash and incomplete of any critic or commentator to fail to take into account the weighty authority of extrinsic tradition.

It is true that on first reading the Apocalypse gives the strong impression of having come from a hand different from that of the author of the fourth Gospel. The distance between them seems considerable, not only from the point of view of language, but also regarding the doctrinal context of the Apocalypse in comparison to that of the Gospel and the Johannine Epistles. However, the more we study these texts together, the sooner we begin to see beyond the superficial appearances, and to see how the gap begins to narrow. The author of the Gospel does not quote the Old Testament as frequently as does the Apocalypse author, who seems resolved to present a sort of Christian re-reading of the ancient texts, especially of the prophecies. As a matter of fact, it seems to us that this one intention of the Apocalypse author to speak the language of the prophets of Israel, should be in itself a virtually sufficient explanation of why the style of the Apocalypse is so different from that of the other texts of the Johannine Corpus. Besides, it is not entirely correct to say that the fourth Gospel is sparing in its references to either the texts or the ideas of the Old Testament; as matter of fact, it has been said that "It is the most Hebraic of all the books of the New Testament, with the possible exception of the Apocalypse" (J. B. Lightfoot, *Biblical Essays*, London, 1893, p. 135, quoted by J. A. T.

Robinson in NTS, Jan. 1960, *The Destination and Purpose of St. John's Gospel*).

The Apocalypse author is proud to call himself a Jew (cf. 2: 9; 3: 9). And it would be entirely erroneous to see the author of the fourth Gospel as an anti-Semite. As a matter of fact, he places much less difference between Gentiles and Jews (unlike St. Paul), than he does between the ideas of light and darkness. If he seems to go hard on the Jewish contemporaries of Christ, it is because he sees them as refusing to see Jesus as their Saviour, and as thereby aligning themselves with the forces of darkness. J.A.T. Robinson (cf. above) says, in the eyes of the author of the fourth Gospel, the real Judaism is that which has recognized Jesus as the Messiah, so much so that to be a true Jew is the same as to become a true Christian. J. A. T. Robinson says (*Jesus and His Coming*, London, 1957, p. 122) that, in the evangelist's eyes, the real Judaism is that which has recognized Jesus as the Messia, so much so that to be a true Jew is the same as to become a true Christian. In saying this, Robinson has not devised a relationship between Apoc. 2: 9 and 3: 9; rather, he has come to perceive the relationship that is really there.

The mystical perception and the love of God in the fourth Gospel seem to be at opposite ends to the terrible God of Jewish eschatology and of the Apocalypse. But even here, we must not fail to see that the God of the Apocalypse is not without love and affection. True enough, the emphasis is upon His absolute transcendence, but this is because the author sees his mission requiring him to recall to his Christian readers the intransigent monotheism of the prophets, in order to make effective his reply to the impious presumption of the Roman emperors, who seek to be adored as divine.

Besides, there is no lack of mystical perception in the Apocalypse, any more than eschatology is lacking in the fourth Gospel (cf. especially Apoc. 3: 10 and 7: 15, if these texts refer, as we think they do, to the present life). Unfortunately, a number of critics (J. Wellhausen, W. Bousset, A. Loisy, logical passages should be extrapolated from the fourth R. Bultmann, E. Hirsch), have proposed that the eschato-Gospel, on the grounds that they are insertions, or even revisions, made by members of the Church for the purpose of bringing the fourth Gospel into conformity with the general frame of mind of the early Christian community. However, such a manipulation of the text is nothing short of arbitrary, and is entirely without support in the earliest manuscripts.

We prefer to follow Lohmeyer, who sees the respective doctrinal contents of the fourth Gospel and of the Apocalypse not as mutually exclusive, but rather as mutually complementary. Notwithstanding the rather common assertion to the contrary, the basic assertion of the Apocalypse author is not the imminence of the Parousia, but rather that the risen and glorified Christ, who will manifest himself at the Parousia, is already present in His Church, protecting it, and, more generally, presiding as sovereign lord over the entire course of human history, leading it to the consummation of the Parousia. Thus the Church has nothing to fear, even from its worst enemies. And this idea of the Church, for which Christ will perform His great work, is already present in the substratum of the fourth Gospel as well.

It is true that some key-ideas of the fourth Gospel are either absent from, or at least little emphasized, in the Apocalypse. Allo seems to have made too little of this fact, which should be explained. Nevertheless, the similarities are at least as remarkable as are the differences, and any really objective study of the unity of authorship should take the one aspect into account no less than the other. Lohmeyer says, correctly, that the basic notions of the Apocalypse, *THANATOS; PHŌNĒ; PEINAN; DIPSAN; NIKAN; MAR-TYREIN*, are clearly Johannine, and that the theme of the living water is common to both the fourth Gospel and to the Apocalypse, and is found nowhere else.

Another particularly noteworthy coincidence is the theme of Christ as pierced or transfixed, which is common to both documents; furthermore, the text of Zach. 12: 10, upon which the theme is built, ("they shall look upon him whom they have thrust through"), is used in both John 19: 37 and Apoc. 1: 7, in a similar translation, different from that of the LXX. Also, if the Woman, the Mother of the Messiah of Apocalypse 12, is first of all the spiritual Sion of the prophets, which eventually becomes the Church, (and can be the Blessed Virgin Mary only secondarily, cf. below), then the Woman of Cana and of the farewell on Calvary is Mary, insofar as she represents the Church, mother of the people of God of the new dispensation.

In our view, authors have not yet accounted sufficiently for the close affinity which unites the fourth Gospel and the Apocalypse. For example: we would search in vain through the Hebrew and Greek Bibles, or even through the Aramaic Targumin, for the origin of the quotation attributed to Jesus in John 7: 38. But the problem seems to vanish, or at least to be less acute, in the light of the parallel text of Apocalypse 22: 1 ff. Here the river of living water is clearly a synthesis of the river which flows forth from the Temple of Ezechiel 47: 1 ff. (cf. Apocalypse 22: 2) and of the living waters which flow from Jerusalem in Zach. 14: 8 (recalled in Apocalypse 22: 3). The strange phrase *EK TĒS KOILIAS AUTOU* of John 7: 38, seems apparently to come from a too material translation of the Aramaic text, according to the quite reliable view of Torrey.

It would be stating the obvious here to insist that the fourth Gospel and the Johannine Epistles can be separated only with the greatest difficulty, from the Apostle John. The only question really remaining before us, therefore, is this: given that the fourth Gospel and the Johannine Epistles on the one hand, and the Apocalypse on the other, could not have come from the same hand, in spite of the many evident similarities existing between them, how can we explain the relation of the two sets of texts, with the same Apostle?

It seems clear that the final redaction of the fourth Gospel should be attributed to someone other than the Apostle St. John. We follow here, almost in its entirety, the opinion offered by Pére Braun, (*Jean le Théologien, et son Évangile dans l'Eglise ancienne,* Paris, 1959), and by G. M. Camps (*Commentaire de l'Apocalypse de Montserrat,* cf. above). It is at best difficult to imagine how a Galilean, formed entirely in the Hebrew manner, could have been the unaided composer of our present Greek fourth Gospel. It seems more credible that John would have preached his message first, and that he would have made some early partial renderings in written Aramaic. This would allow us to retain at least some elements of the hypothesis of an Aramaic original of John's Gospel. As for the final redaction, it could have been done after the death of the Apostle, by one of his disciples, a polished Greek-speaking Jew of the Diaspora community. This would also explain the final section of the Gospel in which the redactor or redactors add a notation testifying to the reliability of the Apostle's Gospel message (21: 24). We could also see in this explanation the reason for the use of the phrase "the disciple whom Jesus loved." Although such a phrase could certainly have been used by the son of Zebedee in person, still it seems all the more credible that it might be due to the high regard in which John was held by the disciple who was the last to have a hand in the redaction of the Gospel after the death of the Apostle himself.

As for the Johannine Epistles, which are closely allied to the Gospel, in spite of clearly evident differences of thought and expression, they could have been written by St. John himself (thus they would be anterior to the Gospel), although John could have availed himself of the services of a scribe, even of the same disciple who later was to be responsible for the final redaction of the Gospel. Père Braun prefers to speak of two distinct redactions, one for the Gospel and another for the Epistles, although this seems to us to explain less well the close relationship which unites these two sets of texts (Gospel and Epistles).

If such is to be taken as the complicated explanation of the origin of the fourth Gospel and of the Johannine Epistles, then the difference between them and the Apocalypse is due to the fact that only the Apocalypse is from the hand of John himself (thus G. M. Camps). We could also follow the thought of Père Braun, that even for the writing of the Apocalypse John used a secretary or redactor, a practice which we know was widespread and common in the milieu of the time. Given this hypothesis, the collaborator who served the Apostle was much poorer in Greek than the redactor who produced the finished text of the Gospel and the Epistles.

In any case, it is the Apostle John who presents the account of his visions. The fact that he foregoes the title Apostle in a work so akin to the style of the ancient prophets, is not at all a valid objection; on the contrary, an anonymous writer who would have wished to present his work as that of the Apostle John, would have been most certain to use the title. To reject the son of Zebedee, in favor of an unknown John the presbyter, whose very existence is doubted by some (Zahn, Gutjahr, Sickenberger, Michaelis, Meinertz, Schnackenburg), would be, as Menoud says, "giving too quickly to a fragile and unproven hypothesis the credence which one would thus refuse to accord to the data of established tradition" (*L'Évangile de Jean d'après les recherches récentes*, p. 78).

Menoud's careful statement brings us to our final point on this question. We admit readily that the last word is yet to be said on the authorship of the Apocalypse. Whatever eventual solution may be adopted, we must never lose sight of the data of tradition. The apostolic and Johannine origin of the Apocalypse is attested by even more ancient tradition than is that of the fourth Gospel, since even Justin attributes the composition of the Apocalypse to John, "one of the Apostles of Christ" (*Dialogue with Trypho, the Jew*, 81: 4). That this John could be John Mark, author of the second Gospel, becomes quite unlikely, given the evidence of the many differences of style and doctrine existing between the two works.

It may seem strange at first glance that the author of the Apocalypse, if he is himself one of the chosen twelve, should seek to glorify the Apostles by showing their names inscribed (21: 14) on the foundations of the heavenly Jerusalem (cf J. N. Sanders, *St. John on Patmos*, NTS 9, (1963), pp. 75-76). But this is, after all, merely a reference to the

will of Christ, who has assigned a position of pre-eminence
to the members of the apostolic college taken as a whole.
Such an exaltation, not of persons as such or of their holiness,
but of the apostolic office, is nothing more than a reflection
of the gospel message itself, which is evident also in the
letter to the Ephesians (2: 20 and 3: 5; cf. Apocalypse
18: 20).

CHAPTER VII

VARIOUS PROBLEMS

1. THE WOMAN OF THE APOCALYPSE

Specialists in the comparative history of religions have always been interested in the 12th chapter of the Apocalypse, and particularly in the opening vision, of the woman who gives birth to the eschatological Savior, and who is pursued by the dragon of hell. Commentators have compared this scene of the Apocalypse with various elements of ancient pagan mythology, of which we think it would be well for us to recall a few here:- there are, e.gr., the Greek myth of Leto, pregnant by Zeus and pursued by the serpent Python (A. Dieterich *Abraxas, Studien zur Religiongeschichte des späteren Altertums*, Leipzig, 1891); the Babylonian myth of Marduk, son of Damkina (the goddess of the earth), and conqueror of the monster Tiamat (H. Gunkel, *Schöpfung und Chaos in Urzeit Und Endzeit, Eine religionsgeschichtliche Untersuchung über Gen. I und Ap. Joh. XII*, Göttingen, 1894; 1921, p. 171-398; there is also the Mandaean application of the Babylonian myth in the history of Manda of Hayye, who struggles against the monster of the black waters before the creation of the world (A. Jeremias, *Babylonisches im Neuen Testament*, Leipzig, 1906, pp. 34-45); some speak of a combined influence of both Iranian and Egyptian myths (Bousset in his commentary, cited in the previous chapters); more often writers speak of a legendary element quite widespread in antiquity (cf., e.gr., the 4th eclogue of Virgil); and of a heavenly Savior who comes to earth (H. Lietzmann, *Der Weltheiland,* Bonn, 1909; E. Norden, *Die Geburt des Kindes, Geschichte einer religiösen Idee,* Leipzig - Berlin, 1931).

Recently, several factors have brought about the production of an unusually large number of profound studies of this 12th chapter. They fall generally into two categories, of quite unequal importance. First of all, there are those which seek to determine the possible relationship between Apocalypse 12 and Hymn number III of the Dead Sea Texts of Qumran. The second group of studies includes the various monographs dedicated to seeking the identification of the Woman, and to ascertaining her relationship with both the Church and with the Blessed Virgin Mary. Most of the studies in this latter group, as might be expected, are from Catholic authors.

A. THE APOCALYPSE AND QUMRAN; APOCALYPSE 12 AND 1 Q.H. III

On the general relationship of the Apocalypse to the literature of Qumram, the following works will be especially helpful: G. Molin *Qumran-Apokalyptik-Essenismus,* in *Saeculum* 6 (1955), p. 244-281; H. H. Rowley, *Jewish Apocalyptic and the Dead Sea Scrolls,* London, 1957; Danielou, *Les Manuscrits de la Mer Morte et les origines du christianisme,* Paris, 1957.

Among the works dedicated to the interpretation of 1. Q. H. III, 8-18 (the hymn really seems to begin a bit before, in 11: 31), some works consider, at least in passing, the problem of the possibility of some connection with Apocalypse 12. Any listing would necessarily include the following, although there are many more: A. Dupont - Sommer, *La*

Mère du Messie et la Mère de l'Aspic dans un Hymne de Qumran, RHR, 195 p. 124-188; J. V. Chamberlain, *Another Qumran Thanksgiving Psalm*, in JNES, 11 (1955), pp. 32-41; J. V. Chamberlain, *Further Elucidation of a Messianic Thanksgiving Psalm from Qumran*, in JNES, 14, (1955), p. 181 sq.; H. W. Brownlee, *Messianic Motifs of Qumran and the New Testament*, NTS, 3 (1956-1957), p. 12-20; 195-210; R. E. Brown, *The Messianism of Qumran*, CBQ. 19 (1957), p. 53-82; M. Delcor, *Un Psaume messianique de Qumran, Mélanges Bibliques redigés en l'honneur de A. Robert*, Paris, 1957, p. 334-340; O. Betz, *Die Geburt der Gemeinde durch den Lehrer*, NTS, 3 (1956-1957), p. 314-326; also by the same author, *Das Volk seiner Kraft: zur Auslegung der Qumran-hodajah* III, 1-18, NTS, 5 (1958), p. 67-75.

Specialists disagree widely on the interpretation of Hymn III of Qumran. The childbirth referred to in the Hymn is certainly metaphorical, which fact alone is a valuable help toward a correct exegesis of Apocalypse 12, insofar as it should be thus less urgent to see this Apocalypse text referring necessarily to the birth of Jesus in Bethlehem (cf. below). On the other hand, however, neither is it certain, as some have maintained (Dupont - Sommer; Chamberlain; Brownlee), that the person who says, "yea, I am in distress as a woman bringing forth her firstborn," is the community, considered under the figure of the Mother of the Messiah, locked in struggle against "them that carry in their womb the seeds of worthless things," or, to use the phrase of Dupont - Sommer, with "the Mother of Satan."

We are inclined rather to follow the idea of O. Betz, that the person suffering the pains of childbirth is really the "Teacher of Righteousness" (who is probably the author of Hymns); he has painfully given birth to the community ("the male child"; "that miracle of might and mind," and stands in opposition to the party of the wicked, led by their chief, "the woman pregnant by the viper."

It has not been really demonstrated in any decisive fashion that this latter expression refers to Gen. 3 (as does the serpent of Apocalypse 12). The phrase seems to be explained better with reference to Is. 59: 4-5, which is quoted directly in Hymn II: 27-28, all the more so since Isaias and the Psalms are the books most quoted in the Hymns of Qumran. Cf. J. Carmignac, *Les citations de l'ancien Testament, et spécialement des Poèmes du Serviteur, dans les hymnes de Qumrân,* in *Révue de Qumrân,* no. 7, juin 1960, p. 337-393. Cf. also the Gospel phrase "Brood of vipers," (Mt. 3: 7; 12: 34; 23: 33). All these elements seem to indicate that the messianic character of the Qumran text is at least doubtful, and that it would be rash to conclude irrevocably to any necessary relationship between it and the text of Apocalypse 12.

In general, we see the great need of maintaining a circumspect attitude in this type of comparative study. Insofar as there are clear similarities (cf. e.gr., the "male child" mentioned in the Hymn, which seems clearly to be borrowed from Is. 66:7), they may reflect no more than the use of common sources, either in the Scriptures, or in the other Jewish traditions; in any case, there is no justification at all for concluding at first sight, that the meaning is the same in each occurrence of the same or a similar phrase.

B. THE IDENTITY OF THE WOMAN OF APOCALYPSE 12

This question has brought out a huge number of studies in recent years. The list which we present here, follows chronological order, but has no claim to being complete.

J. M. Bover, *El cap.* 12 *del Apoc. y el* 3 *del Gen.* in Est E,

I (1922), p. 319-336; L. Fonck, *Signum magnum apparuit in coelo*, VD, 2 (1922), p. 354-357; W. Lampen, *Mulier amicta sole*, in *Studi Francescani*, 20 (1923), p. 273-282; G. Perella, *Senso mariologico dell'Apocalisse XII*, in DTH (Piacenza), 18 (1940), p. 221-225; A. Rivera, *Inimicitias ponam* (*Gen* 3: 15) ... *Signum magnum* (*Apoc.* 12), VD. 1941, p. 113-122; 183-189; L. di Fonzo, *Intorno al senso mariologico dell'Apocalisse 12*, in Mar., 3 (1941), pp. 248-268; G. M. Roschini, *La Donna dell'Apocalisse 12*, in Mar., 4, (1942), pp. 127-128; J. Sickenberger, *Die Messiasmutter im 12. Kapitel der Apokalypse*, in *Tübinger Theologische Quartalschrift*, 126 (1946), p. 357-427; J. Dillersberger, *Das Weib und der Drache*, in *Wort und Wahrheit*, 2 (1947), p. 257-268; J. Bonnefoy, *Les Interpretations ecclésiologiques du chapitre 12 de l'Apocalypse*, in Mar, 9, (1947), p. 208-222; C. Henze, *Un testo dell'Apocalisse*, in Mar, 10, (1948), p. 273-276; J. Bonnefoy, *Le mystére de Marie selon le Protoévangile et l'Apocalypse*, Paris, 1949; R. Murphy, *An Allusion to Mary in the Apocalypse*, in ThSt, II (1949, pp. 565-573; M. Jugie, *Assomption de la Sainte Vierge*, in *Maria, Études sur la Sainte Vierge sous la direction d'Hubert du Manoir*, t. I, Paris, 1949, p. 619-658; D. Unger, *Did St. John see the Virgin Mary in Glory?* CBQ II (1949) p. 249-262; 12 (1950), p. 75-83; 292-300; 405-415; H. Rahner, *Maria und die Kirche*, Innsbruck, 1951, p. 105-115; G. Bissonnette, *The Twelfth Chapter of the Apocalypse and our Lady's Assumption*, in *Marian Studies*, 2, (1951), p. 170-192; J. Kosnetter, *Die Sonnenfrau in der neueren Exegese*, in *Theologische Fragen der Gegenwart* (*Festgabe Innitzer*) Wien, 1952, p. 93-108; J. Gallus, *Scholion ad mulierem Apocalypseos*, VD 30 (1952), p. 334-340; F. M. Braun, *Marie et l'Église d'aprés l'Ecriture*, in *Bulletin de la Societé Francaise d'Études Mariales*, Paris, 1952, p. 14-15; F. M. Braun,

La Mére des Fidéles, second edition, Tournai - Paris, 1954; F. M. Braun, *Eve et Marie dans les deux Testaments*, in *Bulletin de la Societé Francaise d'Études Mariales*, Paris, 1954, p. 9-34; Carlos de Villapadierna, *La mujer de Apoc. 12 es la Virgen Maria?* in CultB, Segovia, 1954, p. 336-345; P. Bellet, *La vision simbolica de la Mujer en Apoc. 12, I,* in CultB, 116 (1954) p. 248-251; J. Giblet, *Mulier amicta sole juxta Apoc. XII*, in C. Mech, 1954, p. 724-726; B. J. Le Frois, *The Woman clothed with the Sun,* (*Apoc.* 12), *Individual or Collective?* Roma, 1954; J. J. Weber, *La Vierge Marie dans le Nouveau Testament*, Paris, Colmar, 1954; A. Colunga, *La mujer del Apoc.* 11: 19 - 12: 18, Salmanticensis, 1954, pp. 675-687; L. Cerfaux, *La Vision de la Femme et du Dragon de l'Apocalypse*, ETL, 31 (1955), p. 21-33; A. Romeo, *La Donna ravvolta dal sole, madre di Cristo e dei cristiani, nel cielo*, in *Virgo Immaculata*, vol. III, *De Immaculata Conceptione in Sacra Scriptura*, Romae, 1955, p. 215-217; *Marie et l'Apocalypse* (author not named), in AmCl, 1955, p. 621-624; F. M. Braun, *La Femme vêtue du soleil*, in Rev Th, 1955, p. 639-659; A. M. Dubarle, *La Femme couronnée d'étoiles* (Apoc. 12), in *Mélanges Bibliques rédigés en l'honneur de A. Robert*, Paris, 1957, p. 512-530; L. Stefaniak, *Interpretacya 12 Rozdzialu Apokalypsy sw. Jana w swietle historii egzegezy*, Poznam, 1957; A. Trabucco, *La donna ravvolta dal sole* (*Apoc.* 12) *nell'esegesi cattolica posttridentina*, Romae, 1957; L. Deiss, *Marie, Fille de Sion*, Paris, 1958, p. 161-208; A. Th. Kassing, *Die Kirche und Maria, Ihr Verhältnis im 12 Kap. der Apk.* Düsseldorf, 1958; B. J. Le Frois, *The Mary-Church Relationship in the Apocalypse*, in Marian Studies, 9, (1958), pp. 79-106; A. Th. Kassing, *Das Weib das den Mann gebar* (Apk. 12-13), *Benediktinische Monatsschrift*, 34 (1958), pp. 427-433. J. Michl, *Die Deutung der apokalyptischen Frau in der Gegen-*

wart, in BZ, 1959, p. 301-310; A. Feuillet, *Le Messie et sa Mére d'aprés le chapitre XII de l'Apocalypse*, RB, 1959, p. 55-86; S. Lyonnet, *Maria santissima nell'Apocalisse*, Tabor (Roma), 25 (1959), p. 213-222; R. Laurentin, *Court traité de théologie mariale*, Paris, 1959 (4th edit.), p. 32-35; P. Prigent, *Apocalypse 12, Histoire de l'exégése*, Tübingen, 1959; M. Peinador, *El problema de Maria y la Iglesia, La interpretación de Apocalipsis XII, I ss.*, in Ephemerides Mariologicae, 1960, p. 161-194; P. P. James, *Mary and the Great Sign*, in Am Ecc Rev, 142, 1960, p. 321-329.

Those contemporary theologians who specialize in Marian studies seem to be inclined at times to go a bit beyond the proper limit, and look to the Scriptures for Marian meanings which will offer support for their theses. In this regard, it seems that many writers forget that the application of the text of Apocalypse 12 to Mary is far from being the oldest explanation of the passage; neither is it the best attested explanation; furthermore it is replete with difficulties. We should state here clearly, once and for all, that the only incontestable exegesis of the passage (cf. the studies of Stefaniak, Michl, Prigent, Trabucco ... listed above) is that which sees it in an ecclesial sense. The Woman whom John contemplates is first and foremost the ideal Sion of the prophets, who, by bearing (metaphorically) the Messiah, becomes the Church. This is the undeniable meaning of the Old Testament passages which the author of Apocalypse 12: 1-6 has used, especially Is. 26: 17; 60: 19-20; 66: 7, and doubtless also Cant. 6: 10, which seems to depend, in its turn, also on Is. 60: 19-20. The application of the passage to Mary thus is not as obvious as it may seem at first glance, although we also think that it is probably correct. This, briefly, is our view of this important and difficult passage.

Placed as it is between the 6th and 7th trumpets, the

tenth chapter of the Apocalypse has described a new investiture of the prophet, and foretold a new series of events, which have to deal with the Christian Church and its relations with the nations, and especially with the Roman Empire. These events proper begin in chapter 12, in which the glorified Christ is saluted, not under the Jewish titles of Lion of Juda, or Root of David (5: 5), but as the one who is to rule the nations with a rod of iron. The Woman, Mother of the Messiah who appears to the Seer, is the people of God of the Old Testament, who, after giving Christ to the world, becomes the Christian people. Her painful childbirth refers to the Passion of Christ, which is the necessary prelude to His Resurrection and to the appearance of the Church. It seems to us, therefore, that the placing of the vision here is perfect; it thus indicates the transition from the time of Israel to the time of the Church.

The Marian aspect of the interpretation must necessarily be in accord with this view of the context. If it is true, as we think it is, that in John 19: 25-27, Mary, whom Jesus addresses as "Woman," sees herself as charged with the metaphorical and miraculous childbirth of the Woman-Sion, which is described especially in Apocalypse 21: 1-6, then the application of this Apocalypse text to Mary is quite correct and normal, especially if we bear in mind at the same time the twofold reference of the Woman, in Gen. 3: 15, and the mother of Emmanuel in Is. 7: 14. We could hold that there is question here of a double birth, that of Bethlehem, insofar as Mary is seen in her own individual and personal role as Mother of Jesus; and that of Easter morning, insofar as Mary represents and gives flesh to the community of the faithful (cf. in this sense J. Comblin, *La Résurrection*, Paris, 1958, pp. 65-66). We would do well to remember here the common occurrence of frequent transition in the Semitic mind from the individual to the collectivity, and *vice-versa;* thus the history of the community is that of the individual, and the deeds of the men of bygone ages (and the consequences of these deeds) are present in the lives of their descendants in the present-day community. Given this fundamental understanding, we can see that an ecclesial exegesis of Apocalypse 12 should not exclude a Marian meaning, as long as this latter element remains restricted to the secondary and subordinate importance which alone is proper to it.

In any case, it is an undeniable fact that the passage from the old dispensation to the new era of grace, the transition from the synagogue to the Church, (described symbolically in Apoc. 11: 1, 2), was effected through Mary: "When the fullness of time came, God sent his Son, *born of a woman"* (Gal. 4: 4). Mary's maternity is completely unique, rooted in the mystery of the Incarnation and in the fact of her being Mother of Jesus. Thus, if there is question of her exercising also a metaphorical motherhood at the birth of the Church on Calvary, this is nothing more or less than the proper extension of her messianic motherhood.

2. THE THOUSAND YEAR'S REIGN AND THE PROBLEM OF MILLENARISM

GENERAL STUDIES

Corrodi, *Kritische Geschichte des Chiliasmus,* Frankfurt - Leipzig, 1781-1783, 4 vol.; V. Ermoni, *Les phases successives de l'erreur millénariste,* in *Révue des questions hist.* LXX, 1901, p. 353-388; L. Gry, *Le millénarisme dans ses origines et son développement,* Paris, 1904; H. Bietenhard, *Das tausendjahrige Reich,* Berne, 1944; W. Nigg, *Das ewige*

Reich. Geschichte einer Hoffnung, Zürich; 1954; J. Dan-
iélou, *Théologie du Judéo-Christianisme, Histoire des doctrines chrétiennes avant Nicée*, Paris, 1957, p. 342-366;
Dictionary articles: H. Leclercq, *Millénarisme*, in *Dict.
d' Archéologie chret. et de Lit.* XI, 1181-1195; A. Michel,
Résurrection, DTC, XIII, 2520-2544; G. Bardy, *Millénarisme*,
DTC, 1760-1763; A. Gelin, *Millénarisme*, SDB, 1289-1294;
W. Bauer, *Chiliasmus, Reallexikon für Antike und Christentum*, XV, 1954, 1073-1078, J. Michl, art. *Chiliasmus*, in
Lexikon für Théologie und Kirche, vol. 2, Fribourg i. B.,
1958, p. 1058 ff.

SPECIAL STUDIES ON APOCALYPSE 20:1-6

J. Sickenberger, *Das Problem des tausendjährigen Reiches
in der Apoc.*, *Festschrift S. Merkle gewidmet*, Düsseldorf,
1292, p. 300-316; H. Höpfl, *De regno mille annorum in
Apocalypsi*, VD 3 (1923), p. 206-210; H. Rongy, *Le millén-
ium de l'Apocalypse XX*, in *Révue ecclésiastique de
Liége*, 23 (1931), pp. 300-307; J. M. Bover, *El milenarismo
y el magisterio ecclesiastico*, in EstB, 2 (1931), p. 3-22;
A. Wikenhauser, *Das Problem des tausendjähringen Reiches
In der John. - Apok.*, in Römische Quartalschrift 45 (1957),
p. 1-25; A. Wikenhauser, *Weltwoche und tausendjähriges
Reich*, in ThQ, 127 (1947), pp. 390-417; D. J. Leahy, *Is the
Millenium or Thousand Years of the Apocalypse the Peace-
ful Expansion of the Church from the Sixth to the Sixteenth
Centuries?* in Scrip. 5 (1952), p. 42-47; A. Colunga, *El
Milenio (Apoc. XX, 1-6*, in *Salmanticensis* 3 (1956), pp.
220-227; J. F. Walwoord, *The Prophetic Content of the
Millenium*, BS 114 (1957), p. 289-307; 115 (1958), p. 1-8;
E. G. Ladd, *Revelation 20 and the Millenium*, in *Review and*

Expositor, 1960, p. 445-466; R. Summers, *Revelation* 20; *An Interpretation*, in *Review and Expositor*, 1960, p. 176-183.

The idea of millenarism, or the hopeful anticipation of a glorious reign of Christ and of the just on earth, derives principally from Judaism itself, in which it appears as a relic of the old terrestrial eschatology, after the later introduction of a more transcendant eschatology (hope for a glorious resurrection and for eternal happiness). The question has also been asked, whether and to what extent the millenarist hope was subject to the influence of Persian eschatology. Cr. E. Cumont, *La fin du monde sélon les mages orientaux*, RHR, CIII, (1931), pp. 29-96.

During the first centuries of the Christian Church, millenarism was popular, not only among some heretical groups, (e.gr. ebionites, montanists), but also, to a greater or lesser extent among some of the principal Fathers, such as Justin, Irenaeus, Tertullian, Melito of Sardis, Hippolytus, Apollinaris of Laodicea, Methodius of Olympus, Lactantius, Commodianus, Augustine (only in his earliest sermons, however). Eventually Augustine rejected the idea (*de Civ. Dei*, XX:7, 9); the Council of Ephesus disowned it in 431. Since then, the notion has persisted almost exclusively within the various small sects, e. gr., the Taborites of Bohemia in the fifteenth century; the Anabaptists in the sixteenth century; the Labadistes (the followers of the French heretic Jean Labadie) in the 17th century; and, more recently among the Darbyites, Mormons, Adventists and Witnesses of Jehovah, in the 19th and 20th centuries.

The followers of the millenarist idea find their chief support in the text of Apocalypse 20: 1-6, which predicts the imprisonment of Satan for 1000 years, and the corresponding reign of Christ and His people, under the title of the "first resurrection." Writers have proposed two entirely opposite interpretations of this text: on the one hand are the millenarists, who believe the passage must be taken in the strictly literal sense (although this has led at times to some explanations which have been little short of absurd); the other outlook, which follows St. Augustine's later interpretation (at first he also believed in a literal reign of 1000 years), sees the text as requiring a properly symbolic and spiritual explanation in keeping with literary structure of the apocalyptic form.

There are also a good number of modern Protestant exegetes (Godet, Zahn, Hadorn, Bietenhardt, Behm, Cullmann, Rissi, Brütsch) who continue to hold in one way or other, to some form of millenarism. However, as a rule, they do not go quite so far as to share the rather exaggerated views of J. A. Bengle (*Gnomon Novi Testamenti, Apocalypsis,* Tübingen, 1942). Even a few Catholics have shown some inclination in this direction (Chabauty, *Études ... sur l'avenir de l'Eglise Cath. selon le plan divin,* Poitiers, 1890; Charles, *Celui qui revient* (Avignon, 1936). In a document dated July 21, 1944, The Sacred Congregation of the Holy Office issued a statement deprecating this mitigated form of millenarism (cf. G. Gilleman, NRT, 1945, pp. 239-241). Nevertheless, Fr. Féret's book, *L'Apocalypse de saint Jean, vision Chrétienne de l'histoire,* which propounds an exegesis quite similar to that of F. Godet (the anticipation of a full flowering of Christian civilization before the end of the world), has never been subjected to any form of censure.

The problem is far from simple. St. Augustine's explanation, which Allo follows, sees the millenium as coinciding with the entire time of the Church; this seems to us to be incompatible with a really objective exegesis of the Apocalypse, in which the millenium has a definitely circumscribed place within the framework of the entire escha-

tological drama. We are more inclined to favor the thought
of Swete, Boismard, and Gelin, (cf. his article *Millénarisme,*
in SDB), who sees the millenium as coinciding with the
renewal of the Church after the passing of the time of bloody
persecutions (which is in progress at the time of the writings
of the Apocalypse), and before the final eschatological
battle to be waged by Gog and Magog.

In a work so strongly influenced by the Old Testament,
especially by the prophetic oracles of Ezechiel (cf. ch. 37,
the vision of the dry bones which come to life), the metaphorical resurrection of the people of God, who were all
but annihilated by the Babylonian captivity, is placed immediately before the attack launched by Gog, king of Magog,
against the Holy Land (chapters 38-39). According to A.
Gelin, the 1000 years reign could be intended, perhaps, as
a reference to the delay preceding the Parousia. Swete sees
it as meaning that the era of the martyrs must be longer than
the era of the triumph of the faith for which they have died.

3. Other Studies on the Apocalypse

In this last section we have presumed to offer collected
references to various studies, which we have had occasion
to mention during the course of our presentation.

A. the text of the apocalypse

The exacting science of New Testament textual criticism
is, of course, a demanding study in itself. For this reason
we have thought it advisable to forego any detailed discussion of this aspect of the Apocalypse. However, for the
sake of contributing, however imperfectly, to the complete-
ness of this study, we list here a few of the more important

works produced regarding this question: H. C. Hoskier, *Concerning the Text of Apocalypse. Collations of all existing available Greek documents with the standard text of Stephen's third edition. Together with the testimony of versions, commentaries and fathers: a complete conspectus of all authorities*, 2 vol., London, 1929 (Cf. RB, 1934, p. 306-308); J. Schmid, *Studien zur Geschichte des griechischen Apokalypse-Textes*, in *Münchener Theologische Studien*, 3 vols., Munich, 1955-1956; (this imposing work, which proposes to consider the text of the Commentary of Andrew of Caesarea, gives a fine resumé, in the third volume, of the history of criticism of the Greek text of the Apocalypse; cf. RB 1956, pp. 583, 585); J.J. Vogels, *Untersuchungen zur Geschichte der lateinischen Apokalypse - Übersetzung*, Düsseldorf, 1920 (cf. RB, 1921, p. 293-294); M. J. Lagrange, *Introduction a l'étude du Nouveau Testament, Deuxiéme Partie, Critique Textuelle, II, La Critique Rationelle*, Paris, 1935; pages 579-625 treat of the Apocalypse; M. J. Lagrange, *Les papyrus Chester Beatty pour les Épitres de saint Paul et l'Apocalypse*, RB, 1934, p. 488-493; H. S. Sanders, *The Beatty Papyrus of Revelation and Hoskier's Edition*, JBL, 53, 1934, p. 371-380; J. Schmid, *Der Apokalypsetext des Chester Beatty Papyrus*, *Neugriech Byzant. Jahrbuch* II (1934), p. 65-108; J. Schmid, *Untersuchungen zur Geschichte des griechischen Apokalypsetextes*, Bib, 17 (1956), p. 11-44; 167-201; 273-293; 429-460; J. Schmid, *Zur Textkritik an der Apokalypse* (13: 10; 18: 2) ZNW, 1950-1951, pp. 112-128; J. Schmid, *Unbeachtete und unbekannte griechische Apokalypsehandschriften*, ZNW, 1961, p. 82-88; F. Mussner, *Neue Studien zur Geschichte des griechischen Apokalypse - Textes*, TThZ, 66 (1957), pp. 50-53; W. G. Kümmel, *Der Text der Offenbarung Johannes*, ThLitZ, 82, (1957), p. 249-254; G. D. Kilpatrick, *Professor*

J. Schmid on the Greek Text of the Apokalypse, Vig. Chr. 13 (1959), p. 1-13; G. Maldfeld, *Zur Geschichte des griechischen-Apokalypse Textes*, ThZ, 14 (1958), p. 47-52. J. N. Birdsall, *The Text of the Revelation of St. John*, EvQ, 33 (1961), p. 228-237.

B. HISTORY OF INTERPRETATION OF THE APOCALYPSE

Attempts have been made by Bousset (*Commentaires*, 1896 edition, pp. 51-171), and by Allo (1953 edition pp. CCXXXV - CCLXXIV), to present a historical conspectus of the history of the interpretation of the Apocalypse. Since the matter is so vast, however, it seems that the best way to attack it would be by parts. The following are such partial studies: W. Kamlah, *Apokalypse und Geschichtstheologie Die mittelalterliche Auslegung der Apk, vor Joachim von Fiore*, Berlin, 1935 (Histor-Studien, 235); A. Wagtel FStn (Münster), 24, 1037, p. 201-259; 305-363 (on Alexander of Bremen, father of the idea of universal history); G. Morin, *Le commentaire homiletique de saint Césaire sur l'Apocalypse*, RBen, 45 (1933), pp. 43-61; A. V. Vega, *Apringii Pacensis Tractatus in Apocalypsim*, Escorial, 1941, S. Bovo, *Le fonti del Commento di Ambrogio Autperto sull'Apocalisse*, Studia Anselmiana, 27-28 (1951), p. 372-403. On the commentary of Tyconius, and the reconstitution of it. Cf. J. M. Gomez, *El perdido commentario de Ticonio al Apocalipsis, Principios de critica literaria y textual para su reconstruccion* in *Miscellanea Biblica B. Ubach*, Montiserrati, 1953, pp. 387-412. On the Apocalypse text commented by Oecumenius in the first half of the sixth century, cf. J. Schmid *Der Apokalypse - Text der Oikumenios*, Bib., 1959, pp. 935-942.

A few more studies of recent history of Apocalypse interpretation are: - E. Lohmeyer, *Die Offenbarung Des Johannes 1920-1934*, ThR, 6 (1934), p. 260-314; 7 (1935), p. 28-62; A. Vitti, *Ultimi Studi sull'Apocalisse*, Bib, 21 (1940), p. 64-78; J. Calès, *L'Apocalypse johannique d'aprés un commentaire récent*, NRT, 49 (1922), p. 341-351; 476-488; E. B. Allo, *Aspects nouveaux du problème johannique*, RB, 1928, p. 37-62; 198-220.

C. OTHER GENERAL STUDIES

E. B. Allo, *L'Apocalypse et l'époque de la Parousie*, RB, 1915, pp. 393-455; J. B. Escande, *L'Apocalypse, document de la Rédemption*. Genève, 1926; C. Clemen, *Die Stellung der Offenbarung Johannis im ältesten Christentum*, ZNW, 26 (1927), p. 173-186; A. Colunga, *Los sentidos del Apocalipsis*, Ciencia Tomista (Salamanca), 1928, pp. 300-331; N. B. Stonehouse, *The Apocalypse in the Ancient Church, A study in the History of the New Testament Canon*, 1929; E. Stauffer, *Das theologische Weltbild der Apokalyptik*, Zeitschr. für systematische Theologie, 8 (1930), p. 203-215; E. Russel, *Possible influence of the mysteries on the form and interrelation of the Johannine Writings*, J. B. L., 1932, p. 336-351; H. E. Hill, *Mystical Studies in the Apocalypse*, London, 1931, Th. Zielinski, *Die griechischen Quellen der Apokalypse, Forschungen und Fortschritte, Nachrichtenblatt der Deutschen Wissenschaft und Technik*, 7, 1931, 155 sq.; Th. Zielinski, *Les sources grecques de l'Apocalypse de saint Jean, Charisteria Gustavo Przychocki a discipulis oblata*, Warsaw, 1934, p. 1-13; C. Clemen, *Visionem und Bilder in der Offenbarung Johannis*, Th St Kr, 107, NF 2 (1936), p. 236-265; C. Clemen, *Dunkle Stellen in der Offenbarung Joh.*, Bonn, 1937; G. Bornkamm, *Die Komposition der apokalyptischen Visionen in der Offenbarung Joh.*, ZNW,

36, (1937), p. 132-149; D. M. Beck, *The Christology of the Apocalypse*, New York, 1942; A. Skrinjar, *Dignitates et officia ecclesiae apocalypticae*, VD, 23 (1943), p. 22-29; 47-54; 77-88; J. G. McCall, *The Eschatological Teaching of the Book of Revelation*, Diss. Southern Baptist Sem. 1948-1949; B. J. Le Frois, *Eschatological Interpretation of the Apocalypse*, CBQ, 13 (1951) p. 17-20; L. Turrado, *Sobre algunas cosas que llaman mas la atencion al leer el Apocalipsis*, CultB, 8 (1951). p. 180-185; J. G. Cepeda, *Para entender el Apocalipsis*, CultB, 12 (1955), p. 353-356; G. Priero, *La Grazia nell'Apocalisse*, Pal. Cl. 35 (1956), p. 703-706; 887-890; 932-937. G. E. Ladd, *The Revelation and Jewish Apocalyptic*, Evangelische Quartalschrift, 29 (1957), p. 94-100; O. A. Piper, *Johannesapocalypse*, RGG, third edit., Tübingen, 1959, 822-834; H. P. Müller, *Die Plagen der Apokalypse, Eine formgeschichtliche Untersuchung*, ZNW, 51 (1960), p. 268-278; E. Schmitt, *Die Christologische Interpretation als das Grundlegende der Apk.*, ThQ, 140 (1960), p. 257-290.

D. MONOGRAPHS

On the introduction and the septet of the letters: R. B. Y. Scott, *Behold He Cometh with Clouds*, NTS, 5, (1959), pp. 127-132; L. Ramlot, *Apparition du Ressuscité au deporté de Patmos (Apoc. 1: 9-20)*, BVChr, 36 (1960), p. 16-25; J. Jankowski, *Actualnosc Apokaliptycznych listow do siedmu kosciolow*, Ruch Biblijny i Liturgicny, 12, (1959), p. 260-277; A. Skrinjar, *Antiquitas christiana de angelis septem ecclesiarum (Apoc. 1-3)*, VD, 22 (1942), p. 18-24; 51-56; J. Giblet, *De revelatione Christi gloriosi in Apoc. I, 9-20*, CMech, 43 (1958), p. 495-497; P. Jouon, *Apocalypse 1, 13*, RSR, 24 (1954), p. 365-366; P. Jouon, *Apoc. 1: 4*, RSR, 1931,

p. 486-487; A. Skrinjar, *Les sept Esprits* (*Apoc*. 1, 4; 3, I; 4, 5; 5, 5), Bib, 16 (1935), p. 1-24; 113-140; E. Schweizer, *Die sieben Geister in der Apokalypse*, EvTh, II (1951-1952), p. 502-512; L. F. Rivera, *Los siete espiritus del Apocalipsis*, RevB, 64 (1952), p. 35-39; A. Skrinjar, *Fui Mortuus, Et ecce sum vivens in saecula saeculorum* (*Apoc*. 1: 18 et 2: 8), VD, 17 (1937), p. 97-106; S. Bartina, *Una espada salia de la boca de su vestido* (*Apoc*. 1: 16; 2: 16; 19: 15, 21). EstB, 20 (1961), pp. 207ff.; P. Wood, *Local Knowledge in the letters of the Apocalypse*, ExpT, 73 (1962), p. 71-78; J. Breuer, *Geheimnis der seiben Sterne, Von Ephesus bis Laodicea, Das Heilige Land in Vergangenheit und Gegenwart* 84, Köln, 1952, pp. 57-62; I. Schuster, *La Chiesa e le sette chiese apocalittiche*, ScCatt, 81 (1957), pp. 217-223; R. North, *Thronus Satanae pergamenus* (*Apoc*. 2:12, 13,17), VD, 28 (1950), pp. 65-76; J. Boehmer, *Tag-und Morgenstern?* ZNW 22 (1923), pp. 228-233; J. B. Bauer, *Salvator nihil medium amat*, VD, 34 (1956) pp. 352-355; J. Alonso, *El sentido de tebieza en la recriminacion a la Iglesia de Laodicea*, Mis Com, 19 (1953), p. 121-130; J. A. Diaz, *El estado di tibieza espiritual en relacion con el mensaje del Senor a Laodicea*, (*Apoc*. 3: 14ss.), Comillas, 1955; J. A. Seiss, *Letters to the Seven Churches*, Grand Rapids, 1955; W. Barclay, *Letters to the Seven Churches*, London, 1957; J. Polanc, *Die Sieben Städten der Geheimen Offenbarung, Eine biblisch-theologische Deutung*, Wien, 1957; A. Jankowski *Manna absconditum* (Apoc. 2: 17), *quonam sensu ad Eucharistiam referatur?* Collectanea Theologica (Warszawa), 29, 1958, pp. 3-10; A. S. Mac Nair, Jr., *To the Churches*, Philadelphia, 1960.

On the first prophetic section (chapters 4-11): A. Rüd, *Gottesbild und Gottesverehrung in Ap*. 4 *und* 5: 5-14, Bibel und Liturgie (24), 1956, p. 326-331; R. R. Brewer, *Revelation*

4: 6 *and Translations thereof*, JBL, 71 (1952), p. 227-231; N. Walker, *The Origin of the Thrice-Holy* (Apoc. 4:8), NTS, 5, 1958-1959, p. 132-133; J. Giblet, *De Visione templi coelestis in Apoc.* 4: 1-11, CMech 43, (1958), pp. 593-597; W. S. Taylor, *The Seven Seals in the Revelation of John*, JThSt, 31, (1930), p. 266-271; O. Roller, *Das Buch mit sieben Siegeln* ZNW, 36 (1937), pp. 98-113; B. Deri, *Die Vision über das Buch mit den sieben Siegeln* (Apoc. 5: 1-5), Wien, 1950-1951; E. Russel, *A Roman Law Parallel to Revelation 5*, Bibliotheca Sacra 115, 1958, pp. 258-264; A. Skrinjar, *Vigintiquattuor Seniores*, VD, 16 (1936), pp. 333-338; 361-368; P. Grosjean, *Les vingt-quatre vieillards de l'Apocalypse. A propos d'une liste galloise*, Analecta Bollandiana, Bruxelles, 1954, pp. 192-212; P. A. Harlé, *L'Agneau de l'Apocalypse et le Nouveau Testament*, Études Théologiques et Religieuses (Montpellier), 36 (1956), pp. 26-35; on the theme of the Lamb, cf. also TWNT, I, pp. 342-345 (J. Jeremias); G. Baldensperger, *Les cavaliers de l'Apocalypse* (6: 1-8), RHPR, 1924, pp. 1-31; J. S. Considine, *The Rider on the White Horse*, CBQ, 6 (1944), pp. 406-422; on the horsemen of the Apocalypse cf. TWNT, III, pp. 338-339 (O. Michel); A. M. Vitti, *Servi Dei nostri* (7: 1-12), VD, 10 (1930), pp. 321-329; A. Skrinjar, *Hi sunt qui venerunt de tribulatione magna* (Apoc. 7, 14), VD, 23 (1943), pp. 115-121; 138-146; J. M. Bover, 144,000 *Signati*, Est., Eccles. II (1932), pp. 535-547; R. E. Murphy, *The Epistle for All Saints* (Apoc. 7: 2-22), Am Ecc Rev, 121 (1949), pp. 203-209; J. S. Considine, *The Two Witnesses of Apoc.* 11, 3-13, CQB, (1946), pp. 377-392; L. Gry, *Les chapitres XI et XII de l'Apocalypse*, RB, 1922, pp. 203-214; E. B. Allo, *A propos d'Apocalypse XI et XII*, RB, 1922, pp. 572-583; D. Haugg, *Die Zwei Zeugen* (Apoc. 11: 1-13), Neutestamentliche Abhandlungen, XVII, I, 1936; J. Munck, *Petrus und*

Paulus in der Offenbarung Johannis, Copenhagen, 1950; OJRA Schwarz, *Die Zwei Zeugen: Kirche und Israel,* Una Sancta 15 (1960), pp. 145-153. On the second prophetic section (chapters 12-22): D. Unger, *Cardinal Newman and Apocalypse XII,* THSt, II (1950), p. 356-367; P. Joüon, *Le grand dragon et l'ancien serpent (Apoc.* 12: 9 *et Gen.* 3: 14), RSR, 17 (1927), p. 444-446; G. Roesch, *Mulier, draco et bestiae in Apoc.* 12: 13 VD, 8 (1928), p. 271-275; A. Monaci, *La fuga dei cristiani a Pella e il sesto Re nei cc. XII e VII del L'Apocalisse,* Roma, 1930, W. Foerster, *Die Bilder in Offenbarung* 12 f. und 17 f. ThStKr, 104 (1932), p. 273-311; J. Rohmer, *L'Apocalypse et le sens chrétien de l'histoire,* RvScR, 1952, p. 265-270 (an explanation of the number 666 of 13: 18 by recourse to Babylonian mathematics); F. Cramer, *Die symbolische Zahl 666 in der Apocalypse* 13, 18, Theologie und Glaube, 44 (1954), p. 63; C. Cecchelli, 666 (*Apoc.* 13: 18), *Studi in onore di G. Funaioli,* 1955, p. 23-31; P. Bellet, *Consideraciones sobre el cap.* 13 *del Apoc.,* XIII Semana Biblica Espanola, Madrid, 1953, 359-379; W. Barclay, *Great Themes of the New Testament, Revelation XIII,* ExptT, 70 (1959), p. 260-264; 292-296; A. Skrinjar, *Virgines enim sunt* (Apoc. 14, 4), VD, 15 (1935), p. 331-339; Ch. Masson, *L'Évangile éternel de Apocalypse* 14: 6 et 7, *Hommage et Reconnaissance, Recueil de travaux publiés á l'occasion du soixantiéme anniversaire de K. Barth,* Neuchâtel - Paris, 1946, p. 63-67; V. Laridon, *Visio Agni cum virginibus in monte Sion,* Coll. Brug. 48 (1952), p. 385-392; P. Miranda, *El Cordero y su Iglesia (Apoc.* 14, 1-5), RevB, 1953, p. 10-15; F. Hommel, Ch. C. Torrey, *Armageddon,* HTR, 31, 1938, p. 238-250; on Armageddon, cf. J. Jeremias in *TWNT,* 1. pp. 467-468; A. Van den Born, Oudtestamentische Studien, 10, 1953, p. 197-203, J. Sickenberger, *Die Johannesapokalypse und Rom,* BZ, 18 (1926), p. 270-282; P. Ketter, *Der römische Staat in der Apokalypse, Trierer Theologische Studien,* 1941, pp. 70-93. On the great Babylon of Apocalypse 17, cf. *TWNT.* 1, pp. 512-514 (G. Kuhn); P. M. Campos, *Roma como corporificaçao do mal na literatura sibilina e apolittica,* Rev. de Historia 1951, p. 15-47; P. G. Skehan, *King of kings, Lord of lords* (Apoc. 19: 16), CBQ, 10 (1948), p. 398; R. Summers, *Revelation 20, An Interpretation, Review and Expositor* 57, 1960, p. 176-183; M. C. Tenney, *The Importance and Exegesis of Revelation* 20: 1-8, Bibliotheca Sacra, 111, 1954, pp. 137-148; J. H. Michael, *A Vision of the Final Judgment, Apoc.* 20: 11-15, ExpT, 63 (1951-1952), p. 199-201; on the image of the Spouse of the Lamb, cf. *TWNT,* IV, pp. 1092-1099 (J. Jeremias). A. Colunga, *El cielo nuevo y la tierra nueva, Salmanticenis* 3 (1956), p. 485-492; D. Yubero, *La nueva Jerusalén del Apocalipsis* 21, I sq., CultB, 10 (1953), p. 359-362; M. del Alamo, *Las medidas de la Jerusalén celeste* (*Apoc.* 21: 16) CultB, 3 (1946), p. 136-138; A. Skrinjar, *Ego sum A et O* (*Apoc.* 22: 13), VD, 17 (1937), p. 10-20.

GENERAL CONCLUSION

St. John's Apocalypse seems nowadays to attract considerably less of the attention of professional exegetes than formerly was the case. This is of course, extremely unfortunate, since the Apocalypse is the perfect crown and finish, not only of the New Testament alone, but also of the entire Sacred Scripture. It is the only book of the New Testament collection dedicated entirely to the task of explaining the Christian meaning of history, which teaching, precious in itself is really no more or less than a graphic presentation of the wonderful way in which the teaching of Israel's ancient prophets has been completely and perfectly fulfilled, in Christ.

We bring this short study to a close with a fervent hope and prayer that scientific research and investigation will continue and develop, so that further knowledge may eventually bring the Apocalypse to occupy the important place which it had long ago, in the attention of bygone generations of Christians. Few books of Scripture had as much of an effect upon the life of the Church as a whole, as the Apocalypse of St. John. One writer has said "The thought and mood of the Apocalypse pervades the entire history of the medieval Church, not only as a source of replies to heretics, or as the secret core of a few sects, but in a broad daylight, and in the general attention of the mass of the people" (H. Focillon, quoted by M. D. Chenu, *La fin des temps dans la spiritualité mediévale* in *Lumière et Vie*, 1953, no. 11 *La Fin du monde est - elle pour demain?* p. 105). St. John's Apocalypse inspired more than countless commentaries. In the Middle ages and later, sculpture and painting, as well as drawings and stained glass, bore out the awareness of its message and brought it to surge within Christian souls. Besides the illuminated decorations on countless manuscripts, the Apocalypse also influenced such art works as the mosaics at the church of Sts. Cosmas and Damian in Rome (6th century); the triumphal arch and mosaics of St. Praxedes (9th century); the paintings in the Church of Saint Savin, Vienne (France); the sculptures and statuary of Fleury-sur-Loire, Saint Benoit-sur-Loire, Saint Nectaire, Souillac, Beaulieu, Moissac; the tapestries of Angers; the stained-glass windows of Saint Martin des Vignes at Troyes, of Chavanges (Aube), and at Ferte-Milon (Aisne); Germany boasts the famous Apokalypsis of Dürer (1498), as well as the works of his disciples and emulators, (Burgkmair, Scheifelin, Holbein). We should also mention *L'Apocalypse figurée* of the outstanding French engraver Jean Duvet, re-printed by Engrammia Press, London, 1963.

This brief resumé is drawn in large part from M. Vloberg's article *The Bible in Art*, in *Guide to the Bible* published under the direction of A. Robert and A. Tricot, (English translation by E. Arbez and M. Mcguire, Paris - Tournai, 1955, vol. II, pp. 547 ff). It would be nothing short of impossible to include here every single case in which themes as elements of the Apocalypse were incorporated into the great Bibles of stone and glass which are the beautiful cathedrals of Christian Europe's classical age (Christ in majesty, scenes of judgment, etc.). Most good historians of Christian art show this development; cf., for example, *Le Christ dans l'art*, in the Encyclopedia *Le Christ*, put under the direction of G. Bardy and A. Tricot, Paris, 1932, p. 879-970. Ch. Brütsch, in his excellent commentary (pp. 286-288) gives a most impressive list, which, however is far from exhaustive, of the countless artistic representations of the Christ in majesty of the Apocalypse which are found in Europe (France, Spain, Italy, Germany and Switzerland). Cf. also W. Neuss, *Die Apokalypse des Hl. Johannes in der altspanischen und altchristlichen Bibel - Illustration*, Münster i. W. 1931; this work offers a carefully detailed study of the miniatures and the manuscripts of Beatus' Commentary on the Apocalypse.

Byzantine iconography also betrays a great influence of the Apocalypse's themes and images. Cf. on this point P. Jerphanion, *Les églises rupestres de Cappadoce*, I-II, Paris, 1925-1932; J. Renaud, *Le cycle de l'Apocalypse de Dionysius*, Paris, 1946; and also L. Heydenreich, *Der Apokalypsenzyklies im Athosgebiet und seine Beziehungen zur Deutschen Bibelillustration der Reformation*, in ZKG, 8, 1939.

There has also been no dearth of fanciful and unreliable material based on the Apocalypse, most of it with a historico-religious nature. Fortunately, most of it has been recognized and denounced by more competent critics. Cf. for example P. Vulliaud, *La Fin du Monde*, Payot, Paris, 1952; H. Marrou, *La fin du monde n'est pas pour demain*, in *Lumiére et Vie*, 1953, no., 11, pp. 77-93. We must understand correctly, not only the idea, but also the profound significance of the frightful and terrible aspects of the millenium theme. Cf. H. Pognon, *L'an mil*, Paris; 1952; H. Focillon, *L'an mil*, Paris, 1952.

Such aberrations, however can hardly be a just reason for

putting aside the riches of this Johannine masterpiece. These errors, after all have almost always been due to the well-intentioned efforts of persons who had little or even no understanding of the laws and stylistic procedures of the apocalyptic literary form. The best policy is, as always, to imitate the mind and practice of the Church, which has consistently rejected these dangerous and misleading interpretations, without losing its reverence for the Apocalypse's intrinsic value. The current renewal of biblical studies will bring about, we are confident, a better understanding of the Apocalypse's essentially symbolic language. As a result of this it should become possible for ever increasing numbers of Christians to benefit from the hidden riches of this sacred and inspired book, and to be free of the erroneous and misguided explanations of it which the unprepared have put forth, to the harm of many.

The Apocalypse is a work of splendor and grandeur, animated by an intense outpouring of emotion and enthusiasm, and written in the face of a truly dramatic and pressing crisis. It is hardly justifiable, therefore, to read it as if it were a cold chronicle foretelling concrete future phenomena. Rather, the properly oriented reader will read it as a magnificent poem, truly inspired, not only in the strictly theological sense of the word, but also insofar as it is the work of exalted literary eminence, replete with imagery and symbolism, many elements of which have become part of humanity's universal literary heritage, such as, e. gr., the opening of the sealed book; the four horsemen; the vision of the redeemed before the throne of God; the Woman; the Dragon; the Harvest; the dirge over fallen Babylon, etc. Usually, ignorance of this poetic character of the Apocalypse has been the underlying reason for false and erroneous interpretations of it. However, it does not seem necessary to follow the poetic structure to such an extent as seeking to discover the meter of lines and strophic values of the syllables, as does Lohmeyer.

The inspired author is truly gifted with an extraordinary power of imagination; he can accumulate the most varied and unexpected images, juxtapose opposites such as light and darkness, chants of praise and shrieks of distress; the radiance of the victorious Lamb and the vile diabolical and human caricatures which seek to deride him. John is fully aware that he is handling the most delicate, and at the same time the most grand and magnificent thing imaginable, the fate of all humanity, contemplated in the light of the redemptive Incarnation. In the light of this stupefying realization, he has availed himself of a literary form full of artifices and conventional images, in order to draw from it a great master-work which his limited dexterity which the Greek language does not at all vitiate (something like the way in which Shakespeare took up a rather bland piece of writing, and transformed it into the immortal *Hamlet* [E. J. Scott]).

The mention of Shakespeare leads us to recall also Dante and his *Divine Comedy,* which was partially inspired in its turn by the Apocalypse, as was also the great English work *Paradise Lost* of John Milton. Of this latter work Scott has said (*The Book of Revelation,* p. 188) "genius has responded to the call of genius."

KEY TO ABBREVIATIONS

AmEccRev	American Ecclesiastical Review (Washington)
AmCl	Ami du Clergé (Langres)
ATR	Anglican Theological Review (Evanston)
BVChr	Bible et Vie Chrétienne (Maredsous)
Bib	Biblica (Rome)
BS	Bibliotheca Sacra (Dallas)
BZ	Biblische Zeitschrift (Paderborn)
BullLE	Bulletin de Littérature Ecclésiastique (Toulouse)
CBQ	Catholic Biblical Quarterly (Washington)
CollBrug	Collationes Brugenses and Gandavenses (Bruges)
CMech	Collectanea Mechliniensia (Malines)
CultB	Cultura Biblica (Segovia)
DTC	Dictionnaire de Théologie Catholique (Paris)
DTh	Divus Thomas (Piacenza)
ETL	Ephemerides Theologicae Lovanienses (Louvain)
EstB	Estudios Biblicos (Madrid)
EstE	Estudios Eclesiasticos (Madrid)
EvTh	Evangelische Theologie (Munich)
ExpT	Expository Times (Edinburgh)
FStn	Franciskanische Studien (Paderborn)

HTR	Harvard Theological Review (Cambridge, Mass.)
JBL	Journal of Biblical Literature (Philadelphia)
JNES	Journal of Near Eastern Studies (Chicago)
Mar	Marianum (Rome)
NRT	Nouvelle Revue Théologique (Louvain)
NT	Novum Testamentum (Leyden)
PalCl	Palestria del Clero (Rovigo)
RGG	Die Religion in Geschichte und Gegenwart, (2nd and 3rd editions - Tübingen)
RSR	Recherches de Science Religieuse (Paris)
RevB	Revista Biblica (Buenos Aires)
RBen	Revue Bénédictine (Maredsous)
RB	Revue Biblique (Jerusalem)
RHPR	Revue d'Histoire et de Philosophie Religieuses (Strasbourg)
RivB	Rivista Biblica (Rome)
RevScR	Revue des Sciences Religieuses (Strasbourg)
RevTh	Revue Thomiste (Paris)
ScE	Sciences Ecclésiastiques (Montreal)
Script	Scripture (Edinburgh)
ScCatt	Scuola Cattolica (Milan)
SDB	Supplement au Dictionnaire de la Bible (Paris)
ThLitZ	Theologische Literaturzeitung (Leipzig)
ThQ	Theologische Quartarlschrift (Tübingen)
ThSt	Theological Studies (Baltimore)
ThR	Theologische Studien und Kritiken (Stuttgart - St. Gotha)
VigChr	Vigiliae Christianae (Amsterdam)
ZNW	Zeitschrift für die Neutestamentliche Wissenschaft (Berlin)

INDEX OF AUTHORS

ALBA HOUSE is staffed by the Pauline Fathers and Brothers. All the operations going into the making of this book were carried out by the Fathers and Brothers as part of their publishing apostolate. The Society of St. Paul was founded to work exclusively in communications. By this is meant that it was instituted to spread the teachings of Christ via the press, radio, motion pictures and television.

PAULINES reach thousands daily—by each book, pamphlet, production — multiplying the good message and carrying it into all manner of places. It is their job in the Church to staff editorial offices, publishing plants, film studios, etc., and to develop those fields of communications still comparatively un-touched for Christ.

PAULINES, aside from living a balanced religious life, perform their apostolic work according to their talents and training as: editors, designers, directors, proofreaders, writers, artists, photographers, pressmen, typesetters, binders, compositors, photoengravers, as well as in many other editorial and technical fields. The **Vatican Council's** decree on the media of social communications has been a great source of renewed energy for them.

INTERNATIONAL as the air-waves, the Pauline Fathers and Brothers are located in twenty-three countries, with headquarters in Rome. In the United States they are in New York City, Boston, Buffalo, Detroit, and Youngstown.

A BROCHURE on the Society and its aims can be obtained for yourself, or any young man whom you feel might qualify to become a Pauline Priest or Brother, by simply sending a card to: The Pauline Fathers and Brothers, Vocation Office, 2187 Victory Blvd., Staten Island, N. Y.